Father–Daughter, Mother–Son

Verena Kast is a practising analytical psychologist and teaches at the University of Zurich. She is President of the International Society for Analytical Psychology has written several books including the bestselling *Loving*.

Father–Daughter, Mother–Son

Freeing Ourselves from the Complexes that Bind Us

Verena Kast

ELEMENT
Shaftesbury, Dorset • Rockport, Massachusetts • Brisbane, Queensland

© Element Books Limited 1997
Text © Dieter Breitsohl AG, Literary Agency Zürich 1994
Original German Publisher: Kreuz Verlag Stuttgart

Originally published as Vater–Töchter, Mutter–Söhne

Published in Great Britain in 1997 by
Element Books Limited
Shaftesbury, Dorset SP7 8BP

Published in the USA in 1997 by
Element Books, Inc.
PO Box 830, Rockport, MA 01966

Published in Australia in 1997 by
Element Books Limited
for Jacaranda Wiley Limited
33 Park Road, Milton, Brisbane 4064

Translated by Matthew Barton
Cover design by Slatter-Anderson
Design by Footnote Graphics
Typeset by Footnote Graphics, Warminster, Wiltshire
Printed and bound in Great Britain by J W Arrowsmith

British Library Cataloguing in Publication
data available

Library of Congress Cataloging in Publication
data available

ISBN 1-85230-940-7

Contents

Acknowledgements

I would like to thank all those who have enabled me to become familiar with an untold number of facets of mother and father complexes. I am especially grateful to those who have allowed me to use the case histories of their complexes as the basis for this book.

Introduction

These days it is common psychological knowledge that people 'have' mother and father complexes. If a man continually wants to be mothered by his girlfriends, it will be fairly obvious that he is suffering from a mother complex. This means that he was somehow unable to loosen at the right time the ties which bind him to his mother, but instead remained stuck at an earlier developmental stage. It is also common knowledge that this is not a healthy state of affairs. He may be called a 'Mummy's boy' or a 'wimp'. Similarly, a man who remains too long under the shadow of his father may be thought of as 'a chip off the old block'; yet the fact that this does not carry a harsh connotation shows us that the son's father complex is seen as more acceptable in our society. A woman who displays a preference for men considerably older than herself is thought to have a father complex – a term which gently reproaches her for not being able to loosen the ties with her father. If, on the other hand, she remains too long with her mother or too obviously imitates her mother's lifestyle, those who feel the brunt of any negative effects of this behaviour will say that she is suffering from a mother complex. It is also quite possible however that such a complex has attractive qualities.

At first sight, then, the nature of these two fundamental complexes seems to be a simple matter, connected as it obviously is with the facts that most people are brought up, formed and influenced by mother and father and that our society looks on the lack of either parent as a serious disadvantage. This concept, at first sight so straightforward, is in fact very complicated and has a direct connection with a human being's whole development. A person's ego complex needs to separate at the proper time from mother and father complexes; then he or she can take in hand the appropriate developmental tasks and form development. A person's ego complex needs to separate at the proper time from mother and father complexes; then he or she can take in hand the appropriate developmental tasks and form a coherent ego or 'ego complex' – a sufficiently strong sense of self. This in turn allows him or her to be equal to the demands of life, to cope with difficulties and to find a certain degree of enjoyment, happiness and fulfillment.

This idea of complexes is central to Jungian psychology. Complexes are specific constellations of memories formed from condensed experiences and fantasies. It is therefore hardly surprising that psychoanalysts frequently characterize their patients by speaking of such things as 'a positive mother complex' or 'a dominating father complex'. These describe fundamental influences which have formed a person's character, in the sense both of the particular difficulties as well as the particular strengths and possibilities he or she may demonstrate as a result. The case histories and descriptions of Jungian psychology contain many references to these complexes. Jung himself provided descriptions of various individual complexes.[1] Yet as far as I know, the mother and father complexes have not yet been fully examined or described. My aim in this book is to do just this. It also seems to me that the concept of complexes can receive new life and relevance from the results of modern studies of infant behaviour. I will not, though, be able to do more than describe the formation of typical complexes. Since no-one is 'only' influenced and formed by a mother complex – for the father complex also always plays a part – and since the ego-complex exerts very variable influences upon the formative complexes according to each individual and specific life-situation, the 'pure' forms of complexes as I describe them are found only very rarely. Nevertheless they give some idea of the character of various specific complex-configurations. The inter-actions of different complexes – which would need to take account of other ones, particularly brother and sister complexes – have been sufficiently described in detailed case studies,[2] and also within the field of Jungian psychology.[3] It is not my aim to connect all the threads of such studies, but to formulate my own view of complexes as it has grown upon me in over 20 years of work with patients, and to stimulate debate and discussion.

A central focus of this study will be the originally positive mother complex: partly because it seems to me that this is too often excluded from consideration, and partly because it has become clear that there exists – in a world decisively formed by the father complex – a longing for values which are inherent in the mother complex, which have been devalued along with the feminine and are now veiled in shadow, but which we urgently need today. Nowadays we far too easily connect the mother complex with the 'devouring mother', thereby unconsciously legitimizing patriarchal, or at least male-centred, values.[4] I do not believe that we should exonerate the inner father-image of the father complex at the expense of the mother-image of the mother complex, as nowadays often happens.[5] I do not wish only to describe these complexes but also to redress the balance as far as I am able to do so.

The complexes themselves have of course come about in a largely patriarchal culture. It might seem that by describing them I am also confirming and perpetuating present conditions. That would be the opposite of my intention. My aim is to clarify these complexes so that we may become aware of their formative influence upon us; so that by naming them, becoming conscious of them, we may ultimately free ourselves from them and become more independent and more able to form better, closer relationships with one another.

CHAPTER 1

Loosening parental ties

'I want to do everything differently'

First, let us take a closer look at the significance of complexes. An originally *positive* complex is one that has had an initially positive influence on a particular person's feeling about life, and therefore also on the development of his or her identity, and will continue to exert this influence as long as an appropriate loosening of ties occurs at the right time.

The originally positive mother complex gives a child the feeling of an unquestionable right to existence, a feeling of being interesting, of being part of a world which will unstintingly answer his or her every need. As a result the ego can relate trustingly to 'another'. The body is the basis for the ego complex.[6] A positive mother complex allows us to experience bodily needs as something 'normal' and satisfy them in a normal way. It allows us to fully enjoy our body, our vitality, our food, our sexuality. The body is free to express emotions and to acccept and integrate similar expressions from other people. An ego that is rooted in this way is capable of stepping beyond its own threshold in physical contact with another, without fear of losing itself. This extends also to emotional intimacy: other people can understand and be understood by us, they contribute to the well-being of our own psyche as we can to theirs. Someone who is assured of interest and understanding, who is given love, care, sympathy and protection, will develop a healthy ego activity.

Not later than adolescence (puberty and post-puberty up to the age of 20), the parents should cease to be regarded as ideal figures. Implicit in such idealization is a devaluing of the child's position. At this age father and mother complexes usually become conscious and a certain separation takes place from the actual parents. But in this process the complexes play a part which should not be underestimated; each form of complex permits particular steps towards separation and forbids others. If leaving or going away has never been allowed, or if it is forbidden to think differently from one's father, then these specific aspects of the complexes will be experienced. The young person will have to set him or herself against them or otherwise fail to achieve separation and freedom. Sometimes it is possible, even when such separation is forbidden, secretly to take from other people what is lacking in the father and mother configuration. But it takes a degree of ego strength to achieve independence in more hidden ways when the open, straightforward way has been forbidden. Some young people simply fulfil their strong urge for independence despite the influence of complexes.

Independence involves a compromise between the needs and requirements of our own life and those of our environment – father, mother, teachers, the society in which we live. Such clearly marked separation phases as adolescence are characterized by feelings of departure and new beginning; they are periods of radical change. The ego complex restructures itself and strives to overcome instability in its feeling of self-worth.

It is therefore important to have had a certain degree of solidarity with our parents even though we must also oppose them. We need the parents we separate from. That is why such problems are caused by the forms of complexes which refuse to allow any separation and which threaten withdrawal of love or denial of a young person's sense of self-worth. Although such parents may provide a safety net which affords a certain protection, this can never replace a loving, painful, honest confrontation with them. Through this confrontation, parents reveal a self-image which the young person has probably never seen before; in opposition to it, he or she can determine his or her own self-image. At such times children sense what remains unfulfilled in the parents' lives and very often make it into an ideal which they wish to pursue. When young people live out what the parents have denied themselves, this sometimes awakens jealousy in the latter. The shadow – everything which has not been lived through, which should have been – is of particular importance in these circumstances.

Adolescents do not however separate only from their parents. They also separate as a whole generation from the previous one. There is a collective shadow which is usually adopted with creative enthusiasm by young people and developed into a whole style and way of life. In the late 1960s and during the 1970s, for example, the children of well-to-do professional people suddenly became 'flower children', imbued with a feeling for music, love and sensuality. Aspects of the positive mother complex suddenly started being collectively celebrated in a world formed by the father complex. We can observe such developments even in the clothes fashionable at any one time. The children of the jeans generation have now developed a taste for designer outfits.

At adolescence, larger-than-life father and mother figures – such as religions provide – can replace the actual mother and father. Religion teachers have noticed that people of this age demand absolute answers to their religious questions, which is easy to understand from the psychological point of view. The young person is absorbed in an identity crisis and seeks orientation. Since guidance can no longer come from the actual parents, parental archetypes and collective value systems are re-awoken. Adolescents may develop an absorbing interest in particular religions, may become deeply involved with teachings according to which they wish to live. In such a transitional phase one becomes 'the child of a higher power'; this stabilizes feelings of self-worth and makes it easier to put boundaries between oneself and one's parents and to do without their care. But what the adolescent experiences as his or her 'very own path' is often actually a general and collective path which will in turn require further processes of separation before a truly individual path can be found. A person's idea of God is subject to development; if we examine any such images from our own life we will notice that they develop and change. A powerful political conviction in adolescence can also be indicative of father and mother complexes projected onto the unfulfilled promises of political programmes. The difference between a 'normal' political engagement and one rooted in complexes becomes obvious when convictions are considered to be holy, when such terms as 'betrayal' are used, and when politics is thought to be a means of healing all ills, rather than simply a way of ordering human society in as sensible and convenient a way as possible. The former view is of course programmed for failure and disappointment.

Male adolescence

In his essay, 'Freud and the Father Complex', Peter Blos formulates an interesting theory about male adolescence.[7] Blos begins by wondering why there is so much rivalry, competitiveness and friction between young men and their fathers. He suggests that this phase is rarely overcome satisfactorily, and that resulting unsolved problems can affect the rest of a person's life. His theory is that this may be caused by aspects deriving from early childhood. The father enables the young child to counteract a state of total dependency on the mother. By so doing he provides support for life-long forward striving, for emotional and physical development. The father supports the child against a tendency to regression, supports him in the fight with the dragon. (Here we encounter the male fantasy that the father preserves the life-instinct.) At puberty, love for the mother is rekindled in the male – in other words, the mother complex is reconfigured to contain elements of the anima (see p. 18 below for an explanation of this term); therefore fear of primal dependency on the mother arises once more. According to Blos, the father is then again needed to support outward-looking and progressive tendencies; the relationship his son had

with him in infancy is reactivated. But this close and loving connection is no longer appropriate, for if the young man remains
his father's son he will not be true to the process of individuation. Therefore he initiates a powerful confrontation with his
father. Blos believes that the more the two men once loved, and
still love, each other, the greater will be the rivalry between
them. In this connection he puts forward a second theory: at
this stage the emerging sexuality of the adolescent is far more
important for his separation from the father than for his relationship with women. It represents the urge to detach himself
from the father.

Blos says little about separation from the mother, which
astonishes me – but perhaps on reflection doesn't. He believes
that if the confrontation with the father succeeds and therefore
ends idealization by the son, the son can then continue on his
way with his father's approval and respect. But, from the point
of view of depth psychology, a separation from the mother and
subsequently the mother complex is also needed. Otherwise the
mother complex with all its implicit expectations would be
transferred to girlfriend and partner. If the young man should
turn his back only on his mother and thereby devalue her, many
aspects of the mother complex and connected anima elements
would also be devalued and suppressed. Everything of a motherly
or feminine nature would then cause him a good deal of anxiety
and would have to be repressed still more.

It is fairly astonishing how various different theories have in
common the idea of the 'devouring mother',[8] and how easily
women themselves accept and adopt this expression. Do they
identify themselves with the image of an aggressor? This phrase
is often used of actual mothers. But it is necessary to distinguish clearly between the mothers of our complexes and our
actual mothers; archetypal figures should not be confused with
the actual human beings we relate to. We know that fears arise
particularly when we repress something. They force us to take
notice of what we have repressed, to deal with something which
is evidently a necessary aspect of our life. One cannot help
thinking, therefore, that devaluing the feminine by believing

that a man has no need of confrontation with the mother and the mother complex in his search for identity actually renders the motherly and female principle far more threatening than it really is. Theories of the 'devouring mother' have all been proposed by men and can be found throughout all schools of depth psychology.

It is particularly interesting that Blos illustrates his thesis by examining Freud himself. Blos takes it as proven that Freud had a very close relationship with his father Jakob, an intense emotional tie that extended into his mature years. Freud writes in letters that he had been the obvious favourite of this forbidding man. He describes his father as 'extraordinarily reckless and of deep wisdom',[9] and his physical appearance as being of heroic proportions, like Garibaldi. He says of himself that he would have been willing to do anything to remain assured of his father's favouritism towards him. Freud's originally positive father complex shows itself in his later life in his almost exclusive, passionate friendships with men, which – as with Jung – he frequently turned into father–son relationships. Jung, 20 years younger, soon felt himself overwhelmed by 'father Freud'. Blos sees this as a transference situation.

Freud had always felt overwhelmed by his own idealized father, whom he had wanted to praise and honour. In 1896, at the age of 40, he lost his father and succumbed to a life crisis. But this death was preceded by interesting behaviour on his part: although his father lay on his deathbed, he went away for a two-month holiday trip. He also missed the funeral because he was at the hairdresser. Freud himself was astonished by this behaviour; as a result he decided to embark on self-analysis. The fruits of this self-analysis appeared in his first book, *The Interpretation of Dreams*. His separation from his father was now unavoidable; he plunged into an identity crisis which he was able to make creative use of – and so psychoanalysis was born.

In the foreword to his book, Freud wrote that it was a 'reaction to the most significant loss in a man's life'.[10] Such a statement can be made only by someone who has retained an absolute and idealized emotional connection with his father. Two years after his father's death, Freud discovered the Oedipus complex; in his interpretation of this, Blos suggests, he overlooked the role of the father. The oracle of the Oedipus legend foretells that the son which Jocasta will bear Laios will kill him. Laios then takes the new-born boy, pierces his feet so that even as a spirit he will be unable to walk, and leaves him on a mountainside. In other words he tries to kill his son. In many interpretations, including Freud's, the fact that the father leaves the son to his fate,[11] is overlooked. When we enter the realm of our own complex we are often determined and ruled by it and are unable to bring objectivity to bear.

After the death of his father, Freud was able to gain independence. At the same time that he stopped idealizing his father, the implicit devaluing of himself, the son, also came to an end. From then on an impressive development began and a period of remarkable creativity.

In this interesting study Blos has clearly shown that our theories have a connection with our complexes. This may also partly explain why the same phenomena are sometimes interpreted and evaluated in many different ways. Blos's theory, for instance, that the adolescent's powerful emerging sexuality serves above all to help him gain independence from the father could explain why human sexuality has such a central position in the theories of Freud.

Psychoanalysis can be seen as a patriarchal field of knowledge within a patriarchal world. Its theories and propositions give little room, if any, to women.[12] In our society women still have difficulty in assuming their rightful human place, let alone in stepping beyond the narrow bounds they have always been confined within, and conquering territory which should be theirs. Women are still too often seen in relation to men or to children. They are thereby deprived of a primal identity; existing only in connection with men, their identity is derived in a secondary way.[13] When we realize that psychoanalysis grew out of confrontation with a domineering father complex, it becomes more understandable that there is practically no place within it for women. Furthermore we can draw upon this realization in psychoanalytic practice: when dealing with very domineering complexes, analysis of the unconscious through dreams seems to help the process of separation and independence. But we must ask ourselves whether the emancipation of the man has gone far enough if in our times women say that it is so difficult to determine the 'place of the woman' within psychoanalysis.[14] May it not be that we still need to reconnect with and integrate the mother complex?

But was it only Freud's personal father complex that made his theory so male-centred? Jung also had a complicated relationship with his father but was fascinated throughout his life by the great mother archetype; his whole psychology owes so much more to a matriarchal line of thought. Yet he described women – when he really wrote about them – only in connection with men. His own concept of individuation should not have allowed him to do this. However, both men were pursuing their research at a time when the *raison d'être* of women was to be nothing more than mothers or daughters. It is up to the women of today to draw attention to the restrictions which are imposed upon them, even in the area of theoretical research, and to reformulate them in accordance with our own psychology, to try to describe the 'place of women'.

Female adolescence

During the girl's adolescence also, father and mother complexes regain importance. The father complex, imbued with related forms of 'animus', stands in the foreground. Qualities and characteristics which have been experienced through the father are transferred to a male friend and/or to intellectual pursuits. Those which were lacking are sought in these same realms.

We can observe that girls go down the path of social integration in one of two different ways: either they find a boyfriend quite early and become involved in a relationship; or else they dedicate themselves to the life of the mind, in which case they can sometimes find it difficult to connect with the body. But the positive influence of the mother complex – even when it remains unconscious – will often allow them to inhabit the body easily and without undue fuss. The world of the mind to which these girls feel drawn can be a fascinating, inspiring realm, imbued with intellectual quest and spiritual experiences, or it can provide an overview of the sum of human knowledge. In either case, sensitivity and intelligence are a prerequisite.

Sometimes both forms of social integration are found in the same person. Both retain the connection to the father complex, and therefore also the unconscious idealizing of the father-principle.

The problem for women is that emancipation from the father complex is not encouraged by a traditional society. A woman fulfils her social role by finding a boyfriend or partner; whether she develops her own identity in the process seems to be of quite secondary importance. An extreme view of this would be to say that our society influences an adolescent woman to believe that she is 'normal' and a real woman even if she has failed to develop her own identity, even when she assumes an identity only by virtue of her connection with a man.[16] In such a case, she will only feel 'herself' through the presence of a man, who can then easily prescribe how she should be, what she should feel and how she should behave. If she should dare to live according to her own ideas, men will no longer think of her as a 'proper' woman. If the opinion of men is important to her, their criticism will either throw her into an identity crisis or compel her to conform once more. The identity crisis offers a chance of discovering herself.

Women who do not develop a primary identity, who do not emancipate themselves from the father complex or confront the mother complex, or who for other reasons do not develop their own identity, often get very depressed when separations occur. When a relationship breaks down, we need to be able to retrieve a sense of self that is independent of it[17] – which is only possible when some degree of selfhood has first been established. Emily Hancock found in her researches that particularly self-aware women were able to find access once more to their 'inner girl', and thus also their true ego, even after years of conforming to the opinions and wishes of others.[18] Carol Hagemann-White draws the conclusion from this that girls who are self-aware and competent often lose themselves at the beginning of adolescence and conform to the image required of them by their environment.[19]

Although this general assertion may be a little exaggerated and certainly not invariably true in each complex-configuration, nevertheless if one asks women about their girlhood, one often hears that around the age of ten their personality was considerably more independent, more clearly expressed and interesting than it later became. As she conforms, the girl loses important aspects of her original self. That would change if girls were praised more for their originality and less for their conformity, if women were viewed not only as an adjunct to men.

It is apparent that women in responsible positions have been very attracted by the father's role.[20] In such women the problem of female adolescence can be clearly observed. Bernardoni and Werder have shown that eight out of ten women with successful careers had fathers who were academics and who brought their daughters up to be self-reliant and independent. Such women described their fathers as being dynamic, active, ambitious and liberal. The father became a role model while the mother was rejected. At the same time, as well, the mother role itself was rejected as too confined, passive and dull. When asked how they had dealt with the identity problems of adolescence, they generally replied that they had learnt and achieved still more than before. They had found that achievement can compensate for identity problems. Nearly all these women were married, which belongs to the picture of the positive father complex. Men are experienced as attractive and reliable. Such women also usually abide by the norms of their society. If it is the done thing to marry, they marry.

That is one form of contemporary female social integration: not to be emancipated from the father complex but to work within the 'father's world', from which success and appreciation are gained. The fact that beneath their role identity their female identity is fragmented becomes apparent when they can no longer draw on the compensation of achievement, or when a separation situation occurs. This necessitates coming to terms with the mother and the specific mother complex.

In our male-orientated world we are all shaped and influenced by father complexes, no matter what form our own particular father complex takes. So it is surely of fundamental importance for women to continually try to come to terms with their feelings about their identity and its fragmentation, to search for their identity in all sorts of different experiences and situations, rather than simply conform to prescriptive theories about its nature. Groups of women should speak of these things together.[21] In response to Christa Wolf's call of 'No place anywhere', women should make heard their need for a life and place of their own. But such a place cannot be determined by others – not by other women and certainly not by men. Each woman must find it, name it and occupy it for herself.

Coming to terms with the mother

If she is to find her own identity, the adolescent woman must confront and come to terms with her mother and the mother complex. If she does not do this, any relationship she has with a partner is burdened not only by her projections of father experiences and the unfulfilled expectations she had of her father, but also with the unresolved expectations and problems connected with her mother.

Emancipation from the mother takes place in complicated circumstances, made more difficult by the fact that it is not encouraged. The aim of such emancipation, though, is not necessarily to break the connection with the mother and achieve an unrelated autonomy. Ideally, the adolescent woman would free herself from her mother in such a way that a new relationship becomes possible, in which the complex-connections of childhood are as far as possible reworked and transformed. Independence is necessary, not as a final separation but with the aim of entering into a clearer, more straightforward relationship with each other.[22]

Each mother also develops a daughter and son complex in relation to her children; this, for some strange reason, is never mentioned! The father does as well. When mothers or fathers speak, worry or complain about their children, we usually think that these are 'real' problems. But complexes are also at work here. Expectations are projected onto children which extend far beyond them as individuals and which change according to the child's age. As adolescents free themselves, their fathers and mothers go through a necessary and overdue process of emancipation from their own parents.[23] It also seems to me – but this would need to be investigated properly – that, by emancipating themselves from son and daughter complexes, parents could make a significant contribution towards helping their children achieve independence.

Nowadays there are also mothers who combine a number of different roles in their life. Sandra Scarr,[24] for example, has shown that daughters of mothers who pursue a career which they enjoy have more self-awareness as women and are far less likely to become dependent upon men, even when they are influenced by a positive father complex. Coming to terms with the mother also proves easier for them, since they do not have to first rehabilitate their mother concept.

In the emancipation of the daughter, though, it is not only her own mother or the role of mother within society that is influential; archetypal images of the feminine, the qualities that are generally considered to belong to the female, also have an effect. We continually encounter the idea that the 'feminine' is something dangerous. The power of the great female goddesses over birth and death, over fertility and barrenness, over love, hate, and all the abundance of life, is frequently projected onto actual individual women. It is wrong to do this, for such projection expresses, above all, a fear of feminine power: a fear which does not ultimately stem from the fact that women are devalued or idealized, but that their true being is not fully perceived or appreciated. No mother can be said to embody death just because she brings a child into a world which it will leave again at death. The adolescent woman, daily bombarded by such images of woman in advertising, film and literature, must feel dangerously ambivalent about the depths of her nature. The male gods are also so much more immediate than the goddesses, although this has altered considerably in recent years. The fact that women have become more aware of a whole spectrum of feminine deities – not only the mother aspect – shows women's need to feel that there is a goddess, rather than just a male god, at their shoulder; that, in other words, it is right for a woman to have a primary identity, not just one derived from a masculine deity. It is important that the archetypal feminine, as it appears to us nowadays, should be constantly described and brought to consciousness. Womankind is then no longer circumscribed by one-sided images of the 'life-giver' and the 'death-bringer'. Instead her being is enlarged to encompass the full heights and depths of female experience embodied in female deities.

The clear signs of this transformation in the collective con-sciousness should give adolescent women the feeling that their identity is grounded in something inherently valuable and self-reliant, something which connects them with vital aspects of life. It should give them the feeling that they can adopt many different roles. As they become conscious of the various forms of the archetypal feminine, they also develop a longing which is closer to their actual lives: to find ideal examples of women who have lived to the full. There are now many biographies of women by women, which answer this longing. These biographies do not simply idealize women or identify them in a general way with female deities – which would merely be another form of derived, second-hand identity – but instead give evidence of the kind of life a woman can lead, give ideas of what one can do with one's own life.

Such examples are the background against which the adoles-cent woman can achieve independence in confrontation with her own mother. The mother provides an image in contrast to which our own identity is conceived. Girls sense the shadow, the unlived life of their mothers; they begin to idealize aspects which never came to expression in their mothers' lives. 'I want to do everything differently from my mother' may of course indicate an originally negative mother complex as Jung described it,[25] yet it is also a phrase which is typical of the process of emancipation. The daughter does not yet have a real centre of her own, but she can at least be 'against' her mother and so begin to define herself.

However, it is not necessary for daughters to hate their mothers in order to make a stand against them. The theoretical proposition that it is necessary derives from the idea that mothers and daughters are identical and that hate enables the necessary separation to take place so that a daughter can discover her own identity.[26] This involves two misunderstandings. Even though both are women, there is no reason why they should be identical or live in some kind of double unity until the daughter reaches adolescence. And even if they are very similar, which is sometimes the case, hate nevertheless does not bring separation but in fact binds people to one another. Those whom we hate probably consume our thoughts just as much as those we love.

Of course it is inevitable that daughters criticize their mothers during the separation process. A mother may well be blamed for not living her life in a consistent way; for allowing her husband and children, perhaps, to occupy all her attention – but then complaining suddenly that she has wasted her life. She may well be criticized for having 'lived a lie', which could well have been caused by her inability to separate sufficiently from her own mother and father complexes. She may also be accused of delegating to her daughter everything she did not succeed in living out for herself. Such delegation is often double-edged: 'Make sure that you have a successful career of your own, but don't neglect to provide me with grandchildren.' To delegate in this way encroaches upon another's freedom and also has a decidedly negative effect on the mother–daughter relationship. It also happens between fathers and daughters, of course, and between mothers and sons. But particularly, it seems, between mothers and daughters.

The increased uncertainty of a woman's role – which in fact opens up immense possibilities – is also apparent sometimes in the contradictory nature of delegation. A mother might say to her daughter: 'Women have a hard time trying to make themselves heard; but that's no reason for you to be too forward.' How should a daughter react to such a dual message? Less openly criticized, yet still painfully observed, is the uncertainty of women in the work-place. Women know that they often do very good work, but they still remain uncertain about its worth. They have a tendency not to be satisfied with what they have done, or to fail to stand up for its value. It is essential that women learn to be proud of the professional work they do. Flaake[27] explains this feeling of inadequacy by suggesting that mothers and fathers neither affirm nor reflect the aspirations of girls in relation to their future careers. Girls are instead too often praised for grace, beauty and good behaviour: it is these qualities which are affirmed and focused upon. Flaake suggests that women should mutually affirm the value of their work among themselves, so as to counteract this lack. That would of course be beneficial, though overcoming jealousy would be a difficult task.

Ideal examples are not the only decisive catalysts in this phase of emancipation and self-discovery, but also friendships with other women – provided the influence of the mother complex allows this. If a woman has been moulded by a very negative mother complex, women, particularly motherly women, will be for her a source of great disappointment and disillusion, and this path will usually not be open to her. Friendships with other women allow us to become self-aware as a woman, to see ourselves through the eyes of another woman rather than only through our own. Women give a reflection to each other, perceive and accept each other. Friendships between women also evoke a quality of experience which I believe can best be described as an 'anima quality': an atmosphere of mutual connection which creates a sense of expansion without threat, a form of erotic attraction that does not require immediate gratification, a fascination with feminine possibilities, sensitivities, etc which can be explored and savoured. In this process, unconscious feminine imagery is awoken through emotions inherent in it, which have much to do with closeness, with the gentle and also wild abandon of intimacy. This imagery opens up different dimensions of womanhood. Originally Jung thought of the 'anima' as the female soul-aspect of the man, corresponding to the 'animus' of the woman. Yet women's need for anima seems nowadays to be very pronounced and is also vital in their emancipation from the mother complex. Sharing experiences and emotions with other women friends – as long as such friendships are not relegated to second place because of social or family pressure to enter into a male–female relationship – is important for developing relationship structures which foster a woman's own sense of self, in which she can be herself. In addition, this awakens her to a more differentiated range of feelings within a relationship context.[28]

This sort of experience allows a new vision of life to crystallize out, one which also facilitates a reconnection with the mother. This occurs usually in a gentle and compassionate form of confrontation, in which the mother is allowed her rights as a separate individual and is understood and sympathized with. Such a reconnection will show a young woman to what extent she resembles her mother and perhaps even shares the same annoying traits, which she can at best learn to handle differently; but it will also show her, in spite of all similarities, that she is a quite separate, different person.

This reconnection could come about in conversations which show the daughter why her mother chose to live her life as she has; and which also give the mother insight into her daughter's aims and aspirations. It may be that the daughter will, sadly, have to accept that her mother views her endeavours with scepticism, or that she is wholly unable to relate to them because of her own past. The efforts at reconnection are a crisis fuelled by disappointment that the original connection between the childhood daughter and her mother, in which they were perhaps one heart and soul, can never be re-created. This crisis may also express itself in disillusion that the hope of building up a close mother–daughter relationship – which has never yet wholly succeeded, but which is dictated by the fantasy of women – proves so unattainable. The best to be hoped for is a good, trusting relationship between mother and daughter, a relationship between two women who know each other well, who value each other and accept that they are different and have different views.

CHAPTER 2

Complexes and episode memories

'There's no point in doing anything'

Complexes[29] group themselves around a particular basic theme and are infused with strong intrinsic emotion. Whenever this basic theme, or the emotion it causes, is stimulated in our life, we react to the situation and interpret it through the complex. We become 'emotional' and defend ourselves in stereotyped ways, as we have always done before. In such a situation, mutual understanding between people temporarily breaks down. Complexes become apparent in our feelings and actions; but they are also revealed in symbols, in which the core of future potential contained within them is emphasized. According to Jung, complexes have an archetypal core; in other words, they form wherever something essential to life is invoked.

Complexes are at the emotional core of our personality; they are called forth whenever the individual has a painful or significant encounter with an outer event or demand in their environment which overwhelms them, or which they do not have the capacity to deal with.[30] From this it is clear that complexes arise in the interaction of infants and children with those who care for them. Early childhood is therefore a time when complexes are particularly liable to be formed. But they can also arise at any time in our lives.

When he described the origin of complexes, Jung had in mind those which cause difficulty to the individual, which are also, of course, the ones which concern us most. But it is conceivable that all significant interactions between child and adult, all interaction between people altogether, can be complex-forming. Our complexes reflect the formative interactions, whether problematic or not, which we have had with other people, including the relationships of our childhood and the rest of our life. They contain the emotions originally connected with them, our defence systems against these emotions, and the expectations arising from them about how life ought to be.

A difficult or significant interaction between two people which involves emotions can therefore form a complex. Every time that a similar situation or event recurs, it will be interpreted in the light of this complex and reinforce it. In other words, people learn that certain situations repeatedly occur and are always accompanied by the same emotions. Complexes reproduce the episodes of our life which are distinguished by a high degree of emotional content.

Our complexes do not simply reflect our parents or brothers and sisters just as they were, or their behaviour just as it was. They seem to be a complicated melting pot of actual experience and fantasy, of frustrated expectations, etc. It can however be observed that when the knot of a complex begins to loosen, memories resurface and give access to our own past. As a result, we develop a more intense feeling for life, we own our ego complex to a greater degree, and experience greater continuity in our own identity.

Our real past is something very mysterious and no doubt impossible to wholly reconstruct. What *can* be reconstructed, according to Jungian understanding, are our complexes: the parts of them which have been suppressed can be raised into consciousness and recognized as emotional nodal points of our life, which cause and have caused disaffection and alienation, and which are the basis of unresolved projections. Yet they are also responsible for stimulating very specific capacities and contain within themselves the potential for further development, a potential expressed in the fantasies they give rise to. The archetypal images which invariably appear when important aspects of a complex become conscious reveal this potential most clearly.

At least as important as reconstructing the past is the analysis of the expectations connected with every complex-configuration; these do not relate only to the here and now of the analytical relationship, but rather to a person's view of their own future. A complex can close the doors to the future and render new experiences null and void. One of the 'complex-phrases' of a female patient of mine, for example, was: 'There's no point in doing anything. I can never say anything when it really matters.' Expectations, longings, visions of the future – if allowed to manifest themselves at all – are cramped into the straitjacket of an immovable past. This means, though, that our own life is barred to us, and we live between a burdening past and a future of anxiety.

The concept of complexes is very similar to that of the so-called RIGs, 'Representations of Interactions that have been Generalized', of Daniel Stern.[31] Stern takes as his starting point the 'episode memory' described by Tulving:[32] the memory of actual events and experiences. Such recalled episodes can be quite banal everyday events, like eating breakfast; or they can be important emotional events – our reaction on hearing of the birth of a child for example. In episode memory, actions, emotions, perceptions, etc are remembered as an inseparable unity, although we can of course focus on one particular aspect, such as the emotions involved. When similar episodes recur – for instance breast, milk, satisfaction – these episodes are generalized. In other words, the child develops the expectation that these episodes will also recur in the same way in the future. Such a generalized episode is no longer a specific memory: '. . . it contains a variety of specific memories . . . It represents the structure of the probable process of the event, based upon normal expectations.'[33] It is therefore clear that this can give rise to expectations which are disappointed. According to Stern, RIGs arise from all interactions. He sees them as the fundamental unity underlying the image we have of our essential self; they give the infant a sense of possessing a central core, which is the basis of identity.

We can make a link between this concept of RIGs and that of complexes. The theory of episode memory can be seen as an explanation of the way all complexes are stored in the memory. It would also explain why complexes are reawoken in particular situations similar to the original formative episodes; and why they can also be reactivated by feelings and emotions which recall or are related to these episodes. The concept of complexes is not relevant to all RIGs, but to those in which difficult situations have been generalized. The idea of RIGs would also confirm the experience that expectations which stem from complex-memories are seldom traceable to a single remembered episode.

Complexes rarely arise from one traumatic situation alone, but are more like a generalized expectation; this tells us that complex-feeling and behaviour results from repeated and similar interactions taking place between a child and other people in its environment. Even if it is possible and important to recall complex-images – for instance that of a strict father dwarfing a tiny infant who longs to sink into the ground to escape him, and who is too terrified to utter a single sound – this precise episode may not actually have occurred, though it remains a powerful image of the complex, of the generalized episode. It is important to bear this in mind because sometimes the images arising through complexes are taken to be a true representation of actual parents; the fantasy images are equated with reality. Of course these episodes do have a connection with the parents' actual nature, which expressed itself in interaction with their child; but they are not simply parallel. This is particularly true of mother and father complexes in general, which we can say are the generalized concepts of generalized episodes connected with the mother and motherly qualities and with the father and fatherly qualities. It would be quite wrong to judge a man or woman on the evidence of the father or mother of our complexes. Complexes arise in interaction, and women and men are not only mothers and fathers. Furthermore, expectations exist within us which are not based on our actual mother and father, of archetypal mothering and fathering.[34] We can view the generalized expectation in the child as a collective potential for fantasy – which initially has nothing to do with the real interaction with parents, but is probably awoken by this interaction.

A further link between RIGs and the concept of complexes is that complexes can arise throughout life and can also be reworked at any stage. Stern sees the formation of RIGs as continuous, developing on all levels of the self throughout life.[35] In this connection there is also a therapeutic consideration which reflects similarities in the two concepts. If we are working with themes from a patient's life which are determined by complexes, we do not have to try to recall the original formative circumstances. It is sufficient to experience one episode that relates to the complex. It is possible, for example, that a problem situation in a relationship, influenced by a complex, reminds the patient in therapy of an earlier situation in childhood that 'feels the same'. This provides a basis for therapeutic work. We do not have to search for the original cause, for every complex-situation contains within it the generalized episode, accompanied by its characteristic perceptions and feelings. Stern lays importance on finding the 'narrative starting-point', the key metaphor.[36] He believes that searching for the 'original draft', beyond which, according to theory, one could not delve further, is an endless process with little chance of success, since there is a major problem in trying to translate pre-verbal episodes into verbal ones.[37]

In the theory of complexes it is important to understand the symbols and symbolic interactions involved. The complex reveals itself in key images – in dreams, for instance, and in the imagination – which can help us become fully aware of the emotions connected with it. In this way we can draw conclusions firstly about our childhood experiences – which helps us to identify ourselves once more with the child and to understand the difficulties and sufferings of the formative situation – and also about the behaviour of the adult involved, with whom, as adults, we often identify[38] and whose role we of course also adopt. We can also draw conclusions about the nature of the interactions expressed in the complexes, and the ambivalent feelings connected with them. If we succeed in perceiving and experiencing the complex-forming encounters in symbolic imagery, more and more episodes that have helped form the complex, that have also led to its transference upon people other than the parent, begin to surface in memory. In the view of Jungian psychology, though, it is important to recognize that the symbolic imagery of complexes contains a psychic energy potential which expresses itself in connected fantasies. Complexes are usually seen as a hindrance, as something that compels people always to react in a certain stereotyped way to situations which need various and differentiated responses. Yet complexes also contain the seeds of new possibilities[39] expressed in symbols.

Everybody has complexes – though Jung suggests it would be more correct to say the complexes have us.[40] At least, our freedom of will ends where the realm of the complex begins; or, to put it another way, the more our emotions are tied up in our complexes, the less freedom of will we have when these complexes are aroused.[41] Complexes are life problems but also an expression of the central themes of our life; they are both developmental problems and themes of our development. They are what determine our psychic disposition.

To sum up: we can describe a complex as the result of unconscious, generalized episodes of difficult interaction, characterized by a common emotion and core of significance (archetype).[42] Every emotion-laden event becomes a complex. Whenever the themes or emotions connected with the complex are roused, the totality of unconscious associations is activated – or in Jungian terms, constellated – together with connected emotions from the whole of one's life and the resulting stereotype defence strategies. The stronger the emotion and its related context of associations, the 'stronger' will be the complex, and the more other psychic factors, particularly the ego complex, will be forced into the background. The degree of influence of a complex in relation to other complexes and to the ego complex can be discovered through the word-association test which Jung developed and which led him to the concept of complexes.[43]

Jung said of the ego complex that it formed the 'characteristic centre' of our psyche, but that it was nonetheless a complex like other complexes. 'The other complexes enter – some more often than others – into association with the ego complex and thus become conscious.'[44] The ground tone of feeling of the ego complex, one's self-awareness, is held by Jung to be an expression of the sum of bodily sensations, but also of all conceptual images which we feel belong to us.[45] The associations connected with the ego complex revolve around the theme of our identity and its development, and our related feeling of self-awareness. The basis of our identity is a feeling of vitality, with which our sense of ego activity is closely connected; a feeling of being alive, through which our ego affects what is around us and ultimately fulfills itself. Vitality, ego activity and self-fulfillment determine one another. As we develop, our ego-activity enables us to become increasingly self-determined, as opposed to being ruled and formed by others. To experience our own identity we need to have clear knowledge about ourselves, about the images we have of ourselves, and to distinguish ourselves clearly from images which others have of us and impose upon us. A precondition for this relatively separate ego complex is that it needs to differentiate itself at the right time from the parent complexes and become ever more independent, so that a person is able to openly embrace new relationships and experiences. Such separation is dependent not only on parent complexes and actual parents, but also very much on our ego activity and vitality. There are children who manage to separate themselves in spite of constricting parent complexes; others barely manage to extricate themselves from complexes which are less compelling. These differences have to do, among other things, with vitality and ego activity.

In general, we can say that if a particular complex does not become conscious, it will be projected onto others. If the ego succeeds in finding access to the complex-process, in taking responsibilty for it and developing empathy with its own predicament, we can often observe that symbols surface which give expression to the complex; but also physical reactions that can be translated into symbols. If these symbols and the fantasies connected with them can be experienced and given form, then the energy bound up in the complex can fully revitalize us and open us to new ways of living and behaving.

Complexes determine us. If, during childhood, we were given care, attention, interest in all that we did, and were embraced by motherly love, then we will be formed by an 'originally positive mother complex'. This will in turn form our expectations of others, of life, of the world – and also, to a large extent, determine our interests. If, on the other hand, our greatest childhood problem was coming to terms with a mother who, for whatever reason, found it difficult to relate to the needs of her child; and if we did not, either, receive devoted motherly care from anyone else, then we will be formed by an 'originally negative mother complex'. If our first significant experiences or painful conflicts were, instead, with our father, we will be formed – depending on whether they were experienced as encouraging or restricting – by a 'positive or negative father complex'. Mother and father complexes are general terms, which nevertheless give some indication of the mood and atmosphere surrounding a person, of the particular important themes at work in their life and of the typical developmental needs and difficulties which they have.

Complexes not only form us, they are also roused into action. A complex can be 'constellated' by a relationship situation which recalls the complex-situation, also by a dream or a fantasy. In other words, we react emotionally in a way which is not related directly to the actual situation. We overreact, for we are not reacting only to present circumstances but also to all situations in our life which so fatally resemble the present one. At such times we also fail to perceive correctly, for we see everything through the filter of the complex and blank out all that does not belong to it. Accordingly, we have a stereotype strategy which we think will help us deal with the situation.

In the constellation of every mother or father complex we can find certain modes of behaviour that originally helped the child establish a good interactional atmosphere with the mother or father or with the family circle in general. These forms of behaviour are retained in adulthood. If we become conscious of them we enable ourselves to decide whether we wish to dispense with them or not.

I have based my descriptions on the notion that mother complexes are primarily formed in relation to the mother and father complexes in relation to the father. We must remember, though, that these personal mothers and fathers also have general, archetypal aspects because they usually aspire, to some extent, to embody the images they have of fatherhood and motherhood. There are of course other people apart from our parents from whom we can receive mothering and fathering. It is also quite possible, for instance, for someone to be given fathering by their mother. But however variable the possible circumstances and scenarios between children, mothers and fathers, certain attributes of all mother and father complexes are to be seen time and time again. We can therefore speak of typical aspects of these complexes. This is clearly connected with the fact that similar interactions arise repeatedly between children and parents and are not simply dependent on the behaviour patterns of an individual child or its mother or father.

In order to show the typical attributes of father and mother complexes, I will use various general examples to describe the formative 'atmosphere' that surrounds people in a number of different complex-configurations, and also look at the cause and origin of each one. Then, in more detail, I will examine specific complex-situations which have typical characteristics, as well as their own individual colouring. In other words, I will try to find the typical attributes in each real and particular instance.

CHAPTER 3

The originally positive mother complex in men

'The world should like someone like me'

'Complexes which are experienced initially as life-enhancing can later prove restrictive if we do not emancipate ourselves from them at the right age. The originally positive mother complex can easily become negative in its effect. The term 'originally positive' describes a typical configuration which can develop in a wide variety of different ways.

'Waiting for the big break' – Balthasar

In order to fully characterize the mother complex, I will describe a rather extreme case.

A man in his 40s, whom I will call Balthasar, entered therapy with me. He described himself as a very sensual man: the senses were of paramount importance in his life. He emphasized this point by stroking the wooden table-top with his fingers in a sensual way, at the same time mentioning that he had, on his way to me, passed a most interesting tree. He described this tree so vividly that I could smell its fragrance in my imagination. He also mentioned that he ate well and enjoyed eating; he had no wish to alter this, even though he was – to put it mildly – overweight and could recognize the potential benefit of indulging himself a great deal less. He sank back comfortably in his chair, which barely contained his bulk.

To begin with he objected to the idea of seeing me only for an hour; he would prefer, he said, to spend half-day sessions in analysis, or even perhaps a whole day at a time. When we discussed the fee – a large part of which would be paid by his medical insurance – he put forward his case for paying the smallest possible amount: I would, he said, gain a great deal from the therapy sessions with him and should therefore, in exchange, be happy to forego some money. This would also enable him to continue to finance his extended holidays abroad.

By this time my interest was well and truly aroused. What a fine example of a mother complex! He responded to my interest in him by telling stories of his travels and describing to me his capacity for pleasure. He gave the impression of someone who knew how to enjoy himself, whose vivacity was stimulated by another's interest and attention. He felt good about himself. When I told him that I wished to abide by my normal one-hour sessions and insisted also on what seemed to me a fair price, he reacted with apparent good humour and sympathy, yet underneath I could see that he felt hurt: 'You are obviously swallowed up by work; I'll just have to take whatever's left over. It's a pity though; you would probably have got a lot out of it.' It is no doubt significant that he expressed his wounded feeling in metaphors connected with food and eating.

Balthasar was very gifted, but clearly had great difficulty in using his gifts. He had begun four different courses of study and training but only completed one of them. He worked as an artist and showed talent in a variety of different media. He was full of interesting ideas but had nothing to show for it apart from a few isolated sketches and 'trial runs'. He was waiting, he said, for the 'big break', which was bound to come sooner or later, as long as he could be patient. He spoke rather scathingly of his fellow artists as 'work-horses' who produced only in 'dribbles' and then held exhibitions and publicized themselves, but who did not have the patience to hold back for the 'big break'. 'I'm interested in so many different things', he told me;

'for a while I pursue one thing, then I get interested in something else. It's inspiring, isn't it, to have so many varied interests?' Each time that he started to tell me about his ideas, he was able, initially, to infect me with his enthusiasm. It became apparent, though, that he was unwilling to concentrate on any one of his abilities; he was convinced that he must pursue everything and integrate it all into his life. He was also incapable of evaluating his own various gifts. He robustly rejected as 'interference' any commentary on his work by fellow artists. He accomplished very little, had next to no work discipline and little structure in his daily life. Although he had ideas which he set about giving form to, he rarely got beyond the stage of an inspired sketch or a few condensed 'notes on a theme'. This, apparently, was enough for him.

He had difficulty in committing himself in relationships. He told me that he had twice been married and that each time his wife had left him shortly afterwards. He himself had never felt the need to marry. 'But of course, that's what women want – and when they want it, they usually get their way . . .' It became apparent that he was unable to stand up to anyone who 'knew what they wanted'. Yet he made enormous demands on his partners – both female and male, for he considered himself bisexual. Women were meant to be fascinated by him and share and enjoy his rich sensuality. They should have a mothering quality, but not look 'motherly'. They should be as 'young and attractive as possible'. Male partners should be decisive, should know how to get on in life, and be clear about what needed doing. Balthasar's relationships with men lasted at the most three months, for the men he chose were, after a while, mostly too structured, anxious, careful or compulsive for him.

Both his male and female partners accused him of failing to live up to initial expectations. Most people experienced him, to begin with, as warm, sensitive, compassionate, comfortable and helpful. These were also real qualities. But when things started to get difficult, he had no staying power. He found all the 'relationship business' too complicated. He thought that one day, perhaps, Mr or Mrs Right would appear on the scene.

At the age of 35 he had a life crisis. He began to feel 'sick of life'; despair, resignation and self-doubt assailed him. The relationship roundabout seemed to him to be spinning faster and faster. He began, increasingly, to be angry with a world which did not nurture him in the way he expected. When I asked him what it was that he expected, he replied: 'The world should like someone like me, should find me remarkable, should give me the space to unfold my talents.'

These attacks of despair became increasingly frequent. Balthasar tried to fend off his depressed moods with alcohol. When this failed, he sought help in therapy. He said that his enjoyment of life was no longer enough to sustain him, that he was suffering from a breakdown, from a crisis in his relationships, from depression and also from an alcohol problem.

'Leaving is a sin'

Genesis of this complex-pattern

We can best describe our early relationship with our mother by recalling a few typical episodes or images. Balthasar can think of many situations which remain vividly in his imagination and memory. When he describes these episodes, they come back to him with great intensity – of smell, sound, sight and, above all, of feeling.

I will select three such images.

- He remembers himself at various ages in the kitchen, together with his grandmother and mother who are both cooking. The father is also there somewhere, drinking. There are quite a few empty bottles lying about; the atmosphere is relaxed, cheerful and chaotic. There are lots of children around – five altogether; Balthasar is the youngest. Friends of the older children are also there. The whole place is warm and loud, and smells of people and food: it's homely and comfortable.
- Balthasar recalls that he 'never' wore clean clothes. The children who sit next to him at school curl up their noses and

ask if his mother can't wash clothes. He replies that she prefers cooking. He smells his own clothes and finds the odour quite normal. 'That's how everyone smells in our house.'

- The children in his family are rather irregular in their school attendance. If they are challenged about this, the parents give illness as an excuse. People also accuse the father of being a drunkard. The family philosophy is that anyone can do what they like within their own four walls. The family does not seem to consider the father's drinking a problem.

The influence of the mother complex is not mediated only through the mother, but also through the whole 'mother-realm',[46] through everything which is experienced as motherly. The mother in this scenario is described as the one who, assisted by the grandmother, is above all concerned with food and cooking. The atmosphere in the kitchen seems like a second womb, offering protection, nourishment and comfort. The father belongs 'somewhere there' as well but seems to have no real presence; his alcoholic stupor is good-naturedly tolerated. This, at least, is how Balthasar remembers it. The family sticks together against an unfriendly world, which makes demands they are unable to fulfil. Any aggression is turned outwards against the world, rather than being used to help the children separate and free themselves from this mother complex atmosphere.

The whole family is formed by an originally positive mother complex, created by a mother who takes care of the nourishment and physical well-being of her children. There appears to have been a great degree of physical closeness between the individual family members and acceptance of the children. When I asked Balthasar if he remembered his mother ever forbidding or denying him anything, he thought about it for a long time and then recalled the phrase: 'Leaving is a sin.' His brothers and sisters resolved this problem by bringing their friends home to the kitchen. When they wanted to have sexual relationships – which in the 1940s and 1950s meant marrying young – they didn't leave home, but brought their partners to live in their parents' house. Occasionally, though, one or other of the daughters-in-law or sons-in-law insisted on independence and achieved it.

His mother died at the age of 65, when Balthasar was 35. His life crisis at that time evidently had a connection with her death. To begin with he thought he would be unable to cope with her loss. He also felt sorry that she had had so little out of life. He considered his father a 'waster' but thought that her sons at least had brought her some consolation. But then he was very much surprised and cheered to discover that one of his sisters had succeeded in creating the same homely atmosphere as his mother. This comforted him a good deal. That he was able to transfer his mother complex so easily to his sister may indicate that his relationship with his mother was not so much a personal one as a general attachment to the motherly atmosphere, to the feeling of unity and protection which she had provided.

Whoever is protected is of course also confined within boundaries. When a child becomes aware of these boundaries, he or she usually looks for ways to step beyond them, to become more independent. This hardly happened in the case of Balthasar or his brothers and sisters, who did not even feel any need to leave home when they became sexually active and got married. Their central problem was encapsulated in the phrase: 'Leaving is a sin.' That was why they were unable to separate themselves at the proper age from the mother complex.

What was the long-term effect on Balthasar of this phrase and all its associated memories and feelings? In what contexts does it now surface, what is its significance for him? We can trace the effect of complexes in our relationships, our projections, our dreams and fantasies.

Balthasar told me that he always felt very hurt if someone he had invited round went home early. When I asked him what he meant by 'early', he replied: 'Before it's over.' I then asked him if he thought that others might perhaps feel it was 'over' earlier than he did. He looked at me in astonishment and said my comment was absurd. It is clear that a situation in which people go away without being given his permission arouses his complex. He reacts as though he has been deserted and forsaken. It is also clear that he identifies with the role which his mother used to play.

So how does this complex-situation take its course? When people leave 'early', he thinks first of all that he has done something wrong. His good mood is spoiled. He feels deserted and rejected by the people who have left. The whole of the next day he feels bad, is unable to work for wondering what it was that he did wrong. Then he salvages his self-respect by such phrases as: 'These people have no feeling for life, they don't know how to enjoy themselves . . .' etc. But even as he re-establishes his feelings of self-worth by devaluing others, he makes use of terms which one can sense are connected with the original complex-atmosphere: 'feeling for life', 'enjoying oneself'.

Another way he finds of coping with this sort of situation is to take to the bottle and get drunk for days, which is followed by a period of depression. That is also a complex-reaction to a feeling of having been deserted. He feels he has been wholly forsaken, even betrayed.

A further complex-reaction occurs when he goes somewhere with other people. He takes care that no-one is 'lost' from the party. He is annoyed when his friends go in and out of shops in an 'undisciplined' fashion. He likes to see that everyone gets something to eat or drink at the proper time. If someone should eat or drink at the 'wrong' time, he feels that the harmony and *joie de vivre* – with which he was so warmly imbued in the kitchen of his childhood – has been disturbed. He is particularly outraged when someone accuses him of behaving like a mother hen. This often happens and it makes him furious. But he has to admit that his mother was also a mother hen and that he bears some resemblance to her in this respect; he is even, perhaps, a little proud of it.

Balthasar, then, closely identifies himself with the mother figure of his mother complex; he keeps everything together, as he remembers his mother doing. He does not react like the child he once was, who was not allowed to leave, but like the mother who stopped him leaving. As long as no-one in his circle tries to be independent, his behaviour is seen as extremely

pleasant: he cares for people's needs, creates a warm atmosphere and provides food at the right moment. But whenever
someone declines his offer of care and attention, he has a
complex-reaction and feels forsaken. He is completely unaware
that his reaction is determined by his complex. He says: 'I do all
in my power to make those around me feel happy and comfortable; but they don't appreciate my efforts. It's obvious that
they can't bear my way of enjoying life.' The fact that he compulsively watches over others, and that he feels so hurt when
they do not allow him to succeed in his efforts, shows that we
are dealing here with complex-behaviour and not just behaviour
that has been learnt or imitated.

It may also be that the influence of this complex makes him
very reluctant to show his artistic work to the public, to sell it,
or to allow it to be subjected to critical appraisal.

Yet within this complex-constellation he can also identify
with the child who is not allowed to leave. In his relationships
with people, he feels that great pressure is being put upon him.
He tries terribly hard to conform to expectations of how he
ought to be. Not to match up to others' expectations feels to
him like being rejected or deserted. Since he very readily projects
his mother complex on others, he has to fulfil many people's
expectations of him. He adjusts himself to others' requirements
without, however, gaining any thanks for it and without suc-
ceeding in recreating the 'us' experience with which he was
rewarded in childhood for not going away. Instead, he deserts
himself by adjusting to others rather than doing what is needed,
which is to be himself in his relationships.

The originally positive mother complex in the therapeutic situation

'A wonderful conversationalist'

When he first entered therapy, Balthasar wanted to have whole-
day sessions devoted to him. He did not wish to be limited; he
wanted long stretches of time in which to spread himself out.

We can sense from this the theme of 'abundance' which is closely connected with the originally positive mother complex. At the beginning of every session he always said that he wanted to talk about everything, but that there was too little time available. Under pressure from this feeling of having too little time, he was often unable to select a theme for discussion, but instead looked at me expectantly, as if to say: 'You decide the topic! Just make it an interesting one though!' If I turned my attention and interest towards him, he would suddenly grow very lively and succeed in being a 'wonderful conversationalist'. It is likely that he had felt the need to earn his mother's and grandmother's interest in him by being entertaining. It annoyed me that he managed to say so little, in so many words and showing an astonishing gift of the gab; or else, that he outlined a problem in the barest telegram style. If I asked him to supply me with more information or to describe his feelings more clearly, he replied: 'Why should I tell you any more? Surely you can understand me without words?' The mode of communication which had been normal in his original family situation was here reconfigured in the analytical relationship. Either long tales were told in a highly entertaining way, but without much communication of information; or else there was an expectation that everyone would understand each other 'without words'.

I deduced from my emotional reaction to this pattern, from my counter-transference, that this mode of communication had made the young Balthasar feel very insecure and also angry. This was repressed though, and his anger and insecurity compensated for by a feeling of togetherness and belonging. Sometimes he told me that he didn't want to go any further with analysis; instead I should give him some uplifting thoughts and a few pieces of good advice for his new relationship. At these times he was projecting his mother's kitchen onto the analytical situation. He wanted us to be nice and comfortable together, and he wanted me to give him some motherly advice. When I suggested that there were connections between the kitchen of his childhood and the present situation, he could see what I was getting at. But he did not agree that anything needed to change; the value of inspiration, he said, was not to be underestimated. And from the point of view of an originally positive mother complex, he was right. The position he occupied within the analytical situation was that of a child within its fundamental complex. If I thought too long about the way I should reply to him, he would ask me if I didn't like him any more. He felt deserted, which for him was the same as losing the love of another person.

He was interested in dreams which could be interpreted in mystical, utopian ways. But he thought the dreams which clearly showed that he needed more awareness and responsibility in some areas of his life were too 'dictatorial'. He was surprised to find that his unconscious could behave in such a reprimanding way.

Two dream themes kept recurring. The first was: 'I don't want things that I can have. I drive to town, see a parking place, but want a better one. But there are no more to be found. I am meant to enter a house, but I'm not sure which one I want to enter. Suddenly everything is shut. I shrug my shoulders, fed up. Those dreams are a drag . . .'

Such dreams were accompanied by feelings of worry and harassment. Balthasar knew of course that he was being asked to make clear decisions even if the best possible option – or parking place – was not available; that it might even be necessary to decide that the available parking place was the best one. Yet his fixation on the mother complex prevented him for a long time from becoming more decisive and from taking more responsibility for his own life.

The second recurring theme was that of being shut in: 'I'm going up in a lift. It stops somewhere, but the doors remain closed. I'm afraid that I will suffocate. I wake up.' These dreams were accompanied by fearful anxiety. A related dream, which also clarifies the lift dreams, is the following: 'Mother puts me to her breast; she is beautiful, soft and warm. I can't breathe, but I'm still just about alright.'

The mother of the dream was not his real mother, but the representative of his mother complex; this suffocated him but

he was 'still just about alright'. Leaving the softness and warmth
was not possible – nor was it, to begin with, absolutely necessary.

'Betrayal – this awful pain'

*How the originally positive mother complex comes to expression
in relationships*

Balthasar had never really committed himself to a relationship.
He was continually taking flight. One possible explanation for
this is that a man with an originally positive mother complex is
constantly searching for the mother-goddess;[47] therefore no
earthly woman can satisfy him. Another possibility is that people with an originally positive mother complex find separations
very difficult. Separations destroy feelings of togetherness
and require a person to redefine and rediscover his or her own
individual self. But in order for this to happen, one must
have successfully freed oneself from the mother complex and
developed a self of one's own. It was clear that even very slight
experiences of separation threw Balthasar into a depression and
made devastating inroads into his self-esteem.

His reluctance to commit himself to other people had,
though, been reinforced by past events. His first relationship
with a woman, at the age of 19, had been, according to him,
very romantic and sensual. He had many sexual fantasies about
her, which simultaneously oppressed and enlivened him. In
order to transform these fantasies into reality, he wanted to
marry and wished, since he had no career or profession, to
continue living with his parents like his brothers and sisters. His
girlfriend made it clear that she did not like this idea, that she
loved him but not his family. She obviously soon found the
relationship too cloying and complained that he was 'eating her
up'. She also once called him a dumpling – he was already
getting fat – and he never forgave her for this. He interpreted
this comment as a betrayal and breaking of trust and felt
crushed.

Feelings of love, and the sexual fantasies connected with

them, help the ego to separate itself from mother and father complexes in a natural way. Love calls up new images in the heart and mind, which for a while upstage the influence of older images. That is why new aspects of the personality can be developed, alongside new emotions and ways of behaving.[48] Even loss of trust and betrayal are not necessarily such catastrophic events. To feel betrayed, often by our father or mother, is an important milestone on the path of individuation. It throws us back upon ourselves. We experience the pain of loneliness, feel ourselves as single individuals rather than as part of a unifying community of people.[49] It is clear that Balthasar experienced this pain of betrayal for the first time in his relationship with his first girlfriend. He mourned and sulked for two years and wrote poems. One of these poems, he remembered, began: 'Girls are like cuttlefish . . .' After a couple of years he met a man with whom he fell a little in love, but he did not enter into a relationship with him. 'I did not want to feel that awful pain again.'

It is a typical characteristic of men with originally positive mother complexes that they expect life to treat them like a loving mother: to nourish and appreciate them, to decide for them what is best. People with this complex-atmosphere approach others with self-confidence, convinced of their own intrinsic value. The others then usually also respond to them in friendlier, warmer, more interested ways than they otherwise might. Our character and our life are very closely connected. But when people believe that the world is their oyster, it is all the harder for them to have to renounce something. The problem is that such people are searching for a partner who will fulfill all their wishes. They are always a little troubled by the thought that their present partner might be preventing them from finding their true soul-mate, the very best partner of all. This causes uncertainty and disharmony in a relationship. And since the power of decisiveness cannot develop while the ego complex is identified with the mother complex, such people seldom choose a partner but are more often chosen.

A further reason for the failure of Balthasar's relationships was his mainly unconscious desire to be loved unconditionally without being called upon to give unconditional love in return. This behaviour – which, to his fury, led some of his male partners to call him 'childish' – is also an expression of the influence of an originally positive mother complex: one can simply lie back and enjoy the overflowing generosity of love which streams towards one. That is the positive aspect. But the problem with it, of course, is that the generosity of love is rarely sustained for long if one partner always assumes the role of a needy child. The originally positive mother complex had in fact become a prison for Balthasar – this was also apparent from his dreams. His predicament can be fittingly expressed by the image of an extended, comfortable womb in which he lived, much of whose appeal was however lost because he was unable or forbidden to leave it.

A mother not only carries a child in her womb; she also pushes it out into the world when the time comes. The fact that she does so is an archetypally feminine and life-enhancing gesture. The good mother first gives her child the sense of being held, nourished, protected; but when the time is right she also pushes him or her away. Balthasar's originally positive mother complex failed to push him out into his own life, into responsibility for himself. That is why, later, it became negative. The life-giving mother of the mother complex, who represents the possibility of experiencing and enjoying the richness of life in all its aspects, who grounds us in a secure feeling for life, has here become a mother whose protectiveness suffocates and 'strangles to death'. The richness of life cannot come to expression. Instead there is an almost unbearable sense of waste and squandering of resources. Enjoyment and pleasure become a cage because they do not lead to anything else; and the feeling of being held and protected becomes a feeling of imprisonment.

In other words: if we do not experience being driven out of the 'mother-paradise' as something not only painful but also freeing, something which enables us to live our own life; and if in the process we avoid all experiences of separation and loneliness, then the reality of death cannot be felt and known, and our life becomes dead as a result. If one were to formulate an overall theme and aim for Balthasar's therapy, it would be this: he must be born. In this connection I have in mind Erich Fromm's phrase: 'Most people die before they have been wholly born.'[50]

Balthasar can attain this aim by committing himself to the analytical relationship. He was ready to do this, was prepared to try. Such an aim can be attained by working through all the complex-constellations.[51] But it is of vital importance in this process to formulate the values underlying each complex-pattern and bring them to consciousness. It would also be unthinkable to work with this man without, sometimes, sharing with him wonderful utopian images and inspired, inspiring stories.

CHAPTER 4

The originally positive mother complex in women

'You can cope with just about anything as long as you've eaten well'

Balthasar had a sister to whom he could easily transfer his mother complex. He told me a great deal about her, and subsequently I had the opportunity to get to know her when she found it necessary to look for a therapist. This made it possible for me to compare two mother complexes evoked by the same mother and family background. Balthasar's sister is three years older than him.

During therapy, Balthasar asked both himself and me many times why his sister had such an easy time of it compared with him. They had both grown up in the same kitchen, surely they must have the same complexes. Now of course that is not inevitably so; his sister might well have been formed more by her relationship with the grandmother or with the father. Yet the fact that Balthasar could transfer his mother complex so easily suggests that they had a similar complex-configuration. According to Balthasar, she must have had an easier time than he did because she was clearly happier: she had a husband, a family and five children. She never got depressed or turned to alcohol. His theory was that women who do not develop beyond the originally positive mother complex have an easier time of it than men.

He is not alone in thinking this. Nancy Chodorow[52] has formulated theories about the different ways in which identity develops in men and women. She believes that girls form the basis of their identity through identification with the mother, whereas boys must develop their identity in opposition to her, must oppose and separate from her if they are to create their male identity. Chodorow also believes that the emphasis on rivalry between men has much to do with the search for and safeguarding of identity. This would suggest that the man who cannot emancipate himself at the right time will suffer from lack of identity, from a poor sense of self, and therefore from an increased susceptibility to all kinds of mental disturbance. The woman on the other hand who does not free herself from the mother complex would still retain the basis of her identity and would therefore be far less disturbed in her sense of self. She would, though, still be mother-dependent and immature.

'Is that all the thanks I get?' – Barbara

Balthasar's sister – I will call her Barbara – fell into a depression and therefore began looking for a therapist. She wanted one familiar both with psychoanalysis and with body-image therapy, one moreover who also worked both in the behavioural realm and in the field of spiritual therapy. She announced these less than modest demands as if they were a matter of course. I asked Balthasar to tell me something about his sister.

Barbara's family live in a spacious house, but they congregate mainly in the kitchen. There is a similar atmosphere there to the one there had been in her mother's kitchen, but everything is much cleaner and tidier. Barbara likes cooking and is good at it. She is also rather plump – which has never mattered to her before, but now suddenly does. Her brothers and sisters often visit her; it is the place where they all like to meet. At Christmas there are often 40 people gathered in her kitchen, which is really only big enough to hold 10. But that is, apparently, 'really comfortable and cosy'. Barbara's husband also enjoys it; he is generally someone who enjoys himself, but also a fairly quiet person. He is capable of laying down the law every now and then, if needed. He is a gardener, very happy with his work. Balthasar, who had great difficulty in 'establishing his career', finds this surprising and admirable.

Barbara appears to be wholly dependent on her husband. She often lets drop such phrases as 'Let's ask Father first'; 'Father will sort it out'; 'Let's wait until Father gets home.' By referring to her husband as 'father', it is clear that she thinks of herself as a daughter, and therefore also as one of the children.

Her depression began when her children all emancipated themselves rather suddenly and left home. This exodus was caused by the father telling the 24-year-old son that he was too old to live with his parents. As a result of this unheard-of intervention, all the children apart from the youngest left home and set up house together. Balthasar says of these children that they are all interesting people, gifted, but rather extravagant and dissolute. He cannot agree with them leaving home. He can understand his brother-in-law's intervention from an intellectual point of view, but thinks it should have come 'later and in a more subtle way'.

It is interesting that the young people can, in fact, create between them enough of a positive mother complex atmosphere to enable them to leave their mother's kitchen and live together elsewhere. This only happened, though, because of the father.

Barbara has reacted to their departure by falling into a deep depression. She has started to sleep badly – she can't get to sleep for ages, wakes up again very early in the morning feeling completely washed out, and then can't get out of bed. She says that life has no point any more, everything is drab and meaningless. She very much regrets not having a 'little one' any longer to pamper and spoil.

Barbara's identity seems closely bound up with her mother. She has the same number of children, she tries to create the same kind of atmosphere in her kitchen. A woman can certainly get by in this way, provided she has a similar view to her mother of what a woman's life should be like. That is also why her brother envies her. The fact that she has reacted so drastically to separation from her adolescent children may be an indication that she identifies very largely with the mother aspect of her originally positive mother complex, and that it is now high time for her to develop beyond it. Her identity is not, though, bound up with her mother's role as wife. Whereas her mother married a man with an alcohol problem, Barbara's husband is a motherly father figure. She probably had little experience of the 'fatherly' aspect of her father; and now she has managed to marry someone who has a close connection with the feminine. Even if he is a little idealized by his brother-in-law, he is nevertheless a man who earns his living by working with the natural world. To care for the growth and cultivation of nature requires motherly qualities. Yet he is also aware of the need for order and structure; he does not frighten everyone by overdoing it, but he does demand a minimum of order, which has a calming effect on things. It is quite likely that this man is imbued with an extremely well-balanced father and mother complex, and that he feels happy with a positive mother complex atmosphere as long as it does not get out of hand.

Barbara was therefore able to find herself a partner who could not only cope with her complex-configuration but could also complement it. But, according to Balthasar, Barbara was not exactly like their mother: she was torn between letting her children hang on her apron strings and making them more independent, for she felt that her mother had kept them on too short a rein when they were children. Nevertheless she was similar to her mother. Food was also very important to her. Her favourite phrases were: 'You can cope with just about anything as long as you've eaten well'; and 'Get something good inside you and then we'll sort things out'. Like her mother, she knew how to create a sensual, erotic, comfortable atmosphere. She also found it hard to endure separations. Her depression after the over-hasty departure of her children – over-hasty because it had been put off for too long – shows us that she is still rooted in the idea that 'leaving is a sin', even if it is perhaps more hidden in her case than it was with her mother.

It is easy to understand her depressive reaction. Until then, Barbara had drawn her identity in large measure from identifying with the mother aspect of her originally positive mother complex. She had, as a child, experienced an almost archetypal form of mothering. Her own identity beyond the 'mother role' had seldom if ever been called upon with unavoidable urgency. Now, though, she cannot escape being thrown back upon herself. Her depression is asking her to find herself. She complains that she has spent her whole life 'filling hungry mouths' and what thanks has she had for it? They've just gone and left her! Such phrases are typical of a depressed person. But she does not feel 'caged' or 'trapped'. She feels, rather, that she has reached a zero-point and must somehow begin again. She must stop being a mother and establish a new kind of relationship with her husband. When she gently reproaches him for his comment to their eldest son, he tells her that he now wants to enjoy life with her alone, to live with her without children. This clearly expresses his need to be a partner, not just a father.

If we compare Balthasar and Barbara it is obvious that Barbara really has had a much more satisfying life than her brother. Yet she has neither explored nor developed her talents; she has, until now, thrown in her lot with domesticity.

'It will all sort itself out somehow' – Agnes

A 40-year-old woman, whom I will call Agnes, begins therapy because her husband wants to separate from her. As well as a husband she has also had a boyfriend for the last eight years. Her husband believed for a long time that this was a platonic friendship. Now that he has realized that this is not so, he wants to leave his wife. They have two children. Agnes completed her university studies and has been working for some time in her chosen field.

Agnes dresses in a fanciful way. Wherever a scarf or veil could possibly be attached, it is. She speaks with a sing-song intonation, somewhat reminiscent of a little girl. She makes a whimsical, slightly capricious, 'girly' impression, but is also friendly and warm. She seems like a pleasant, easily surprised child. She tells me, wide-eyed with anxiety, that her husband has outbursts of hatred towards her. She can't understand why that should be – she has only good intentions, she doesn't wish to hurt or harm anyone. Why hatred now suddenly? Her husband, she says, is of a ratherly motherly kind and somewhat obsessive. He always calls her 'my lovely child'. She used to find this term of endearment attractive, but now she thinks it is misplaced.

Her boyfriend, whom she met nine years ago, and with whom she has had a relationship since then, treats her more like a woman. He is also very sensitive, but less motherly, more equal, brings her out of herself more. She does not wish to do without either of her two men; she loves them both and neither minds the other, according to her. She also has close contact with her dead mother's old friends, whose company she very much enjoys. And her best friend is a woman with whom she spends much time and who fills an important place in her life. Agnes invests a great deal of time and energy in relationships. Like Barbara she is very capable of enjoying herself, though in her case it is less through food than through relationships and the stimulation they bring. She does not see why any one of her relationships should hinder or exclude any other. It is just her husband who says that they can't go on like that. She herself sees no reason for making any decision about it. She dislikes making decisions and does so only very rarely – usually at work, where it is sometimes unavoidable. At times her husband has criticized her for this and been quite unpleasant about it.

Her husband has now left her, after long, involved discussions about the situation. She is slightly bemused to find herself suddenly alone with two children. She is also astonished to discover how many things she must cope with, now that she is alone. She begins to see that, although she has always been very generous and carefree about money, she must start budgeting a little. Until now, her husband has always taken care of such things. She hasn't even really known how much she earns. She also recognizes that she is not good at bringing up children. She says she is really like a third child who must now suddenly look after the other two. But then she adds: 'It will all sort itself out somehow.' As I listen to her I begin to be really very concerned about her situation; but she is so convinced that everything will be alright in the end that she manages to convince me as well.

Agnes is very interested in art. Literature and the pictorial arts inspire her. She can talk enthusiastically and at length about such things. She frequently makes connections between the images of her dreams and those in great works of art and is pleased to discover such connections. They affirm for her that everything is inwardly connected with everything else in the world. She feels herself to be part of a larger whole and is interested in the way she is interwoven with and related to it. She has vivid dreams and is good at observing and describing her inner world. She is close to her unconscious and very sensitive to other people, and interested in spiritual things. She exudes an atmosphere which makes life seem to be there for the taking, in all its rich abundance; which also seems to suggest that it is pointless to make too much of an effort, for then one might fail to see that life simply provides for one's needs.

She also does not wish to deny herself anything: instead of making difficult decisions she would rather just give herself over to enjoyment. She projects the benevolent 'Great Mother' onto the world and is astonished when people do not behave according to her complex-derived expectations. She has retained a remarkable degree of innocence for her age. Sometimes I ask myself whether she has actually been living in this world at all. She never thinks badly of another, wishes to know nothing bad. She has no shadow; that is to say, she knows astonishingly little about it.

Sometimes she gets annoyed that people try to 'patronize' her. This happens of course because she allows herself to be spoiled and made a fuss of, which usually also involves letting others tell her what to do. But she keeps quiet about her annoyance. Her work is running smoothly. She has been working in the same job for 13 years and finds it interesting on the whole.

How has she become what she is? She married when she was 25 – her mother expected it of her. She had found the kind of man she needed: a motherly man who was also capable of bringing order and structure into her life. He also made all her decisions for her. Then her boyfriend appeared on the scene; she felt that life had granted her everything that she needed, and more. Whereas her relationship with her motherly husband was clearly a father–daughter one, she can be a partner with her boyfriend. This more equal relationship may be a sign that she has moved on a little from the mother and father complex. It also seems to be time for her to make some decisions one way or another. This makes her feel helpless: 'I'll have to watch out that I don't fall into a big hole.' To avoid this happening, she attends lectures, goes to art exhibitions, meets up with people who can be relied upon to hold stimulating and inspiring conversations with her. It is clear that she could become depressed, could 'fall into a hole', which for her means boredom, inability to deal with life, and loss of trust in the world. But she steers clear of the hole. She can let herself be inspired and then she feels alive again.

'Just be the little one and you'll be fine'

Origin of this complex-configuration

Agnes's parents separated when she was four years old. The father faded out of the picture, dying quite young. Agnes did not consciously experience her father's death. She remembers above all the intimacy she shared with her mother, who was protective and loving and made a fuss of her. Her mother was the source of all good, nourishing her both physically and spiritually. Her mother had boyfriends, but Agnes did not feel excluded. She realizes now that she must have been excluded to some extent if her mother was involved in a loving relationship with someone else, but she certainly did not notice this at the time. When the other children at nursery school spoke of their fathers and asked her about hers, she always replied with pride:

'We've got boyfriends instead' – a clear sign of how close she was to her mother.

One memory: she is about six or seven and is sitting on her mother's lap. Her mother is reading to her. They are sitting very close together and Agnes hears her mother's heartbeat. She asks: 'Can you hear my heartbeat too?' She can see this scene vividly in her imagination; she can also smell the fragrance of her mother. The whole image is surrounded with a circle of light, as if illuminated by a spotlight. She knows, though, that they never had such a spotlight, only normal lamps. The illumination must therefore be an expression of their close intimacy. She also tells me that she used to sit on her mother's lap even when she was much too big and heavy; and sometimes, when she was older still, she took her mother upon her own lap. Her mother always had something interesting to say, she was good at engaging and amusing her daughter, and it never occurred to Agnes to question or upset her mother's way of doing things.

Her mother died three years ago. Immediately after her death, Agnes felt destroyed; she couldn't understand why she had not died as well. Then her mother appeared to her in dreams. She took this as a clear indication that her mother was still alive, although in the other world. It seemed to her that it was unnecessary and patriarchal to make such clear and sharp distinctions between this world and the other: it was her task, as a woman, to repudiate such clear-cut distinctions.

Agnes's experience is typical. The dead can appear in our dreams with great force and clarity; usually, though, they seem somewhat altered – they often appear younger. Many people interpret these dreams as a sign that the dead person still lives in some form, and many try to find some access to the 'other world'. But, as the process of mourning continues, it becomes apparent that these images of the dead are in fact inner creations of our own.[53]

But Agnes did not wish to see it like that. She continued to feel deeply united with her dead mother. For her, even death brings no separation. 'The dead live with us; my mother can watch over me even better from the other world.' But when the process of separation from her husband began, her grief about the death of her mother could no longer be avoided; it became a serious and pressing problem.

Agnes found it hard to think of any phrases which might have pointed to possible conflict situations between her and her mother. There simply weren't any, as far as she could recall. But we eventually discovered a lead, in her professional life. She had told me that she usually allowed others to decide things for her. Recently though, she had noticed that her colleagues had often come up with solutions and ideas for her that suited them but were not beneficial to her. In the past they had somehow taken better care of 'the little one', which was their teasing and affectionate name for her. These episodes at work led us to the discovery of a complex-phrase: 'Just be the little one and you'll be fine'. This suggested that she should not grow 'big', and by extension, of course, that she should not leave home. Agnes has been limited to her role as daughter. Even when she relates to her children and needs to play the role of mother, she behaves like a daughter – even to the extent of letting her son boss her about. Her daughter has noticed this and is furious about it; she has temper tantrums, which are a reminder to the mother that she should become more adult.

If this complex-phrase – 'Just be the little one and you'll be fine' – prevented her from developing out of the role of daughter when she was young, then one wonders of course what reaction Agnes's mother had to her marriage. That must surely have been a kind of 'leaving'. Agnes shrugs her shoulders and denies this: 'We were all married'. In other words, all three of them – herself, her husband and her mother – were involved in the marriage. Her relationship to her mother was not affected. Her mother and her husband got on very well with each other. She could therefore marry and still remain a daughter.

Agnes is an unusually friendly patient. She brings very interesting 'material' to her therapy sessions and can also connect it to her everyday life; she is, though, much more interested in the 'eternal' aspects of her dreams. She assumes the role of a daughter who is glad to learn and who has interesting ideas. I frequently experience my own desire to say to her 'You really ought to do this, or that . . . ', but I manage to keep a hold on such reactions. She would be astonished at my energetic way of tackling her problems and would probably fail to understand it. Sometimes I can sense in my feelings the shadow aspects of herself that she has shut off. I then find it difficult to leave her rosy vision of the world undisturbed; I become furious with her passive aggression. I can explain to her what is occurring between us. My anger is an attempt to make her more inwardly active. She can understand this, would also like to change and become more decisive, would like to experience her own anger, because it would benefit her own life – but also because she wishes to do me a favour.

We work at grief therapy. I try to rekindle her awareness of her relationship to her mother and to her husband, and to show her that in both cases something fundamental has altered. Her dreams are very helpful in this process. She also has dreams which have less to do with this grief. She often dreams about houses: for example, she searches for a house in which she would like to live. She finds it very hard to decide. Sometimes there are women living in these houses who are all 'more mature' than she is; she doesn't know them, but she would very much like to. These mysterious, intriguing, unknown women are compelling aspects of the anima: they offer her the possibility of developing, of freeing herself from her fascination with her mother. Her dreams are directly confronting her with what she needs, and, as it were, shaking her awake: she is looking for a house of her own – a space and protected place for the unknown, fascinating, feminine aspects of her psyche. Her own psyche is in fact providing her with the help she needs to separate from her mother.

Anima and animus help us free ourselves from parental complexes. This occurs less through our direct work with these complexes and their manifestations in our everyday life than through us allowing new impulses from our psyche – and there-fore, often, new preoccupations, new 'fascinations' – to take hold of us.[54]

Unprepared for loss and separation

Comparison of the two complex-configurations

Barbara and Agnes were both, for some considerable time, secure in their female identity; it provided them with a good sense of themselves and made them feel fulfilled and 'at home' in their lives. They were each, in their own way, able to enjoy life. Both of them had satisfying relationships, until separations from people who meant a lot to them became unavoidable. Separations always involve more than estrangement from other people; they also inevitably require us to redefine our identity. We are forced to draw back from our connection with another and reconstitute our individual sense of self. This usually involves emancipation not only from the one we are separating from, but also from our parent complexes or from the role images that society has planted within us.

Barbara closely identifies with the mother-role of her originally positive mother complex, yet assumes the position of daughter in her relationship with her husband. Agnes has become a mother also, as if that were quite straightforward for her, but she has still remained far more attached to the daughter role. There are substantial areas of her life which she retains for herself, which she does not allow to be taken from her. The daughter role leaves more options open than the mother role. It is also probable, though, that Agnes's mother stimulated her daughter's interest in much wider and more differentiated ways than Barbara's mother.

Descriptions of the anima are often connected, in the literature of psychology, with four types of womanhood: those of Eve, Helen of Troy, Mary and Sophia. No woman, of course, can be wholly equated with one of these types. One could say, though, that Barbara's mother probably tended more towards the 'Eve type', whereas Agnes's mother was more reminiscent of the others. Agnes's mother was also more obviously influenced by a father complex than Barbara's. Both women have a tendency to become depressed in the face of loss; Agnes, however, can draw upon her own sources of well-being. It seems that she has transformed and integrated the loving, affirming, motherly care that her mother gave her. She does not simply pursue the same interests as her mother; she has cultivated much broader interests. But from her mother, and from the good atmosphere her mother created, she received the certain knowledge that she could draw upon a good feeling about herself when times were bad. The complex-nature of their relationship had a certain obsessive quality; but for Agnes this had a beneficial effect, since her obsession did not demand anything of her which was not suited to her personality. Mothers who bring about an originally positive mother complex in their children are probably distinguished by the fact that they do not – at least in the early developmental stages of their offspring – force anything upon them which is not already present in their character. What is noticeable about Agnes is that she is cut off from her own shadow. This is all the more remarkable because she is, as a well-read woman, familiar with the concept. She freely admits that she is more or less incapable of experiencing or sensing her own shadow. But she has not split it off in such a way as to remain good while others are seen as bad, although there are some hints of this in the relationship with her husband. She is, by virtue of the originally positive mother complex, generally well-disposed to everyone; she does not believe that anyone could intentionally wish her ill.

CHAPTER 5

Live and let live

Typical characteristics of originally positive mother complexes

It will by now have become obvious that it is not easy to characterize the typical aspects of originally positive mother complexes. For one thing, these complexes do not arise only in interaction with the mother but also in relationship to various other adults. Yet even when the mother was the main focus, and the influence of others was only marginal, mothers are still very different from each other; each has her own particular complex-constellation. Balthasar's mother must certainly have been formed by an originally positive mother complex. Her chosen sphere of activity was focused upon nourishment, comfort and protection. Other mothers, such as Agnes's, create a secure feeling of closeness by telling stories. Still others base their intimacy with their children on shared activities. Such mothers succeed – in whatever realm they feel at home in, which in turn depends on the fundamental form of their own complex-influence – in creating the 'us' feeling, a feeling of security. They succeed in communicating to the child that he or she is important and interesting. This also gives the child the feeling that life is abundant and nourishing, that it upholds and affirms her or him. Such mothers will only be able to help their children separate from them at the proper time to the extent that they themselves have learnt to cope with separation, with loss and letting go. If they can do this, their children will benefit from an originally positive mother complex that also allows them to free themselves when the time is right.[55]

A further difficulty in characterizing what is typical of the originally positive mother complex is that not only mothers influence its formation. There exists what one could call a 'mother-realm', in which motherly qualities are experienced. Animals, plants and our whole surroundings are drawn into this realm. It seems to me that the originally positive mother complex is formed in interaction with nature and the things in our environment, or at least projected onto them.[56] This mother-realm includes various people we encounter, the atmosphere we grow up in, our brothers and sisters, father, grandparents and anybody else with whom we live.

According to Mechthild Papousek, modern research into infant behaviour suggests that there is very little difference to be found between the way a father or mother relates to their child. The similarities outweigh the gender-determined differences – which of course do exist.[57] We can therefore infer that central aspects of the mother-realm are also provided by the father.

Furthermore, the fact that various different people can contribute to the formation of different aspects of the mother complex can prevent it from becoming too narrow or constricting. A father's influence can increase the variety of themes and values active in the mother-realm, thereby enlarging and extending it.

Over and above the effects and influences of complex-formation, every person is also driven by the urge to develop and become independent. We can therefore find people whose ego complex has substantially freed itself from the originally positive mother complex. Most of us work upon ourselves, try to change ourselves. We encounter aspects of ourselves in relationships, for example, which make us want to change. The fact that we are all at different stages of development, and that most of us are influenced by more than one kind of complex, makes it difficult to describe the typical characteristics of complexes.

In general, though, people formed by an originally positive mother complex all subscribe to the saying: 'Live and let live', or possibly even: 'Enjoy and let others enjoy'. For them, life is good and right, as are they themselves. They open themselves up to a world which they trust; they expect things to go well and their expectations are often fulfilled. They show a fundamental faith[58] in the world, often too much so. 'It will all sort itself out somehow' is a typical feeling expressed by such people. Their confidence in life can also become a kind of laziness, an assumption that other people will look after their needs. They tend to want to enjoy 'everything', to have their cake and eat it, to have all their desires fulfilled. They therefore often gravitate towards theories which focus upon 'wholeness'. The mother-realm, and with it the mother complex too, is formed from earliest infancy on and is therefore active at a pre-verbal stage. Although it may remain a formative influence throughout all the stages of life, its atmosphere is essentially connected with earliest childhood. As such, it relates particularly to our bodily well-being and to our ability to feel secure in our physical contact with others; and consequently to be open to intimacy of all kinds. It is characteristic of the originally positive mother complex that all the physical expressions of the child are accepted and affirmed – not only the clean and pleasant-smelling ones. People who have therefore experienced life as a 'Great Mother' who cares for them usually have a relaxed and positive relationship to physical existence. They tend to be close to their own senses, to sensual experience in its broadest terms. It is too one-sided to connect the originally positive mother complex with oral experience and enjoyment only. Such people have the capacity to enjoy things on many different levels. They tend to have a close, intuitive connection with the unconscious. They are often imaginative and creative people, whose potential, however, is not always fully realized. They can also be unrealistic and impractical, in which case their potential is merely an unfulfilled promise. To ground ideas in reality takes persistence, which is a form of aggression; it also requires a capacity for self-denial and for tolerating setbacks. If the ego complex is unable

to emancipate itself from the originally positive mother complex, the boundaries of the ego fail to become clearly defined.
When this is the case there is also a danger of impulsive and
uncontrolled outbreaks of all kinds of emotion.

When conditions are right, though, the people formed by this
kind of complex are friendly, accommodating and also sympa-
thetic. They love everything to be harmonious; they thrive on an
'oceanic' feeling in which the interconnectedness of all things
can be experienced, and in which the differences between
people are resolved or overlooked. A shared experience of life's
abundance is important to them,[59] which creates a feeling of
unity and love. This feeling arises for them when they attain
what they consider to be 'everything'.

A general description of the atmosphere surrounding the
originally positive mother complex – both in women and men –
throws up similarities with descriptions in Jungian psychology of
the anima experience,[60] as expressed in images of the mysterious
and attractive stranger. People whose dreams reveal an anima
figure, or who project an anima figure upon a real woman, say
that they experience a deep, oceanic feeling and a longing for a
melting of boundaries, for an absolute union that can never be
achieved. This longing can express itself either in a more sexual
or a more spiritual way. Usually it is a desire for unbounded
physical union, which however is not experienced as 'only'
physical, but as 'wholeness'. According to Jung's theory, anima
and animus are in fact formed under the influence of mother and
father complexes[61] and contain, particularly on an archetypal
level, the aspects which are lacking in the original complexes,
providing a stimulus for development away from them.

The originally positive mother complex provides the ego with
a feeling of being good in a good world, of having an unquestionable right to existence; it gives one the right to love and be
loved, to be respected, to express physical and emotional needs
and to have them met – simply because one exists. It gives one
the right to fulfil oneself, to have a share in the abundance of
life. It gives a feeling of being 'carried' by life. This feeling has
been described by Haerlin as one of 'partaking in life' as

opposed to that experienced by the ego that is compelled to achieve because 'it is not a good ego'.[62]

Neither separation nor decision

Difficulties and problems

The main difficulty encountered by people with an originally positive mother complex is that of separation: the necessity of accepting the existence of death, of recognizing and dealing with separation and new beginnings. A further and connected difficulty is posed for them by the need to make decisions – in favour of something and therefore against something else – and to make use of aggression in their lives.

This does not mean that they are not aggressive. They are capable of taking what they want, for they see the abundance of life as theirs by right, and this can strike us as an aggressive quality. If they do not succeed in assessing their own self-worth in a more moderate, relative light, and if they believe that they are a remarkably special gift to the world, then they will also expect to be treated accordingly. When this does not happen, they are easily offended or hurt. They can become 'difficult', grumble and moan a great deal, and fall into depressions in which their aggression is directed against themselves. They can be self-destructive – usually in an indirect way; they may take substances which seem to promise them the oceanic feelings they believe are their birthright, feelings which they think will deliver them from the 'evils of the world'. Such people can also strike one as passively aggressive: they don't listen properly, forget important things 'by mistake', arrive late . . . The difficulties become more pronounced when, instead of an ego identity appropriate to their particular age, such people have a complex-identity. This manifests either as an identification with the generalized mother of the mother complex – usually based upon the mother as 'great goddess' in her various aspects – which frequently involves illusions of grandeur, or as an identification with the 'eternal child', or with both these alternately.

But the identity problems posed by this form of complex are different for men and women. Men may appear too 'soft' and motherly – although this is of course the judgement of a patriarchal world; it is not necessarily a negative thing if men become softer and more closely connected to their feelings. Or they may seem, even at an advanced age, to be rather boyish. Women who identify themselves with the mother role, on the other hand, are less conspicuous. But they can also appear girlish and behave more like daughters than one might expect of adult women.

The common themes, then, that we find in cases of this type of complex are that people are held back in their development, are hindered from living their own life in a way appropriate to their age, are prevented from being themselves. The process of emancipation is not only not encouraged or supported by the mother figures in their lives but, worse still, is actively discouraged and branded as 'bad' or 'wrong'. There are various reasons for this: people who are themselves dependent find it very hard to encourage their children's autonomy. If the children, in addition, serve to maintain a parent's idealized self-image, then they will be needed to prop up this self-projection for as long as possible. Children enable their parents to re-create the longed-for feeling and atmosphere of the originally positive mother complex. This is a feeling of abundance and wholeness that is stimulated by an accepting, caring, sharing relationship with children. It is understandable that it is not so easily relinquished.

The process of emancipation is also hindered when people fail to accept and integrate their own aggression. They then use it to protect themselves, to shut themselves off from life instead of getting to grips with the world.

A promise eternally unfulfilled

The positive mother complex and depressive tendencies

This form of complex, if it is not resolved through a further process of development, is the basis of depressive tendencies. The ego complex fails to evolve sufficiently; the ego remains too inactive, and its boundaries with other people are too undefined. Characteristic also is a great need to be accepted and loved. If this need is not satisfied, such people will try to gain it through their achievements. They attempt to meet the demands and requirements of the world, although they are in fact furious that life does not behave in a more accommodating and caring way towards them. But they do not dare show this anger, as it separates them from the world. Therefore they turn it against themselves. They are plagued by guilt, believing that it must in some way be their own fault that life is not so wonderful as it once was. Pressing – though also repressed – feelings of guilt arise because they feel themselves to be full of unfulfilled promise, having failed to come up to the high expectations that they and others have of them. This failure is, on the surface, compensated for by illusions of grandeur; they are waiting for the 'big break'. But they have underlying feelings of guilt, which, together with the uncertain focus of the ego complex and the aggression which is neither sufficiently accessible nor manageable, lead to outbreaks of depression. These guilt feelings have a deeper purpose. They remind us that we owe ourselves and our own development something, that we are failing to live our own life with sufficient determination. If we do not find fault with ourselves, we may believe that we are living our life to the full when we are in fact acting under the influence of unconscious and generalized father and mother complexes. Our identity is then not our own but a generalized identity.

In such a scenario, in which the ego complex fails to emancipate itself sufficiently from the mother complex, we can also observe a tendency to anxiety attacks. Fear and anxiety arise in psychological development in the transition from symbiosis to individuation, from dependency to independence, from obedience to responsibility, from unconsciousness to increased consciousness, and from union with others to a greater degree of self-definition. These transitions – with which all pathological states of anxiety are connected – determine whether we become autonomous, whether we find ways of using our aggression, or whether we repress it and do not manage to develop beyond symbiosis. Jung defines fear as an expression of 'the personality's developing aspect' which is held back and hindered from partaking in life and therefore causes fear and is transformed into it.[63] The step from symbiosis to individuation, from unity with the mother to a pleasurable experience of oneself as independent and self-reliant, is a form of separation. Our early childhood experiences of separation determine how anxious we will become, how easily we will cope with separations later in life and to what extent we will be able to be ourselves. But all further separations also continue to determine whether we learn to cope with fear, whether we can take control of our lives in spite of it.

It may be surprising to realize that an originally positive mother complex can be responsible for depressive tendencies and states of anxiety; also for 'narcissistic phenomena' such as illusions of grandeur, over-sensitivity to others' opinions, the need for much attention, together with depressive moods when attention is not consistently given. A coherent, well-defined ego complex is not formed by parental care and attention alone, but by the parents permitting and encouraging – or at last not hindering – ego activity, in the sense of separation and self-discovery. Depressive tendencies and attacks of anxiety are an indication that the self has not asserted itself enough, that a person has not taken sufficient responsibility for his or her individuality. People formed by an originally positive mother complex retain, it is true, a memory of their unquestionable right to existence; but they also suffer from the feeling that the process of individuation necessitates the loss of a wonderful state of unseparated wholeness.

Some of the underlying themes and conflicts which characterize and accompany this kind of complex-constellation, are: separation and unity, abundance and emptiness, life and death, the impossible and the attainable, contemplation and active participation in life.

Sorrow turns to joy

The mother-goddesses – a digression

Jung started out from the idea that the consciousness of the infant is only 'poorly developed',[64] that it therefore does not directly experience the actual mother so much as a 'primal image' of her.

> The mother is . . . an archetypal figure; she is experienced in a more or less unconscious condition – not as a well-defined individual, but as the mother archetype, resonant with a wealth of significance. In the further course of life, this primal image fades and is replaced by a more conscious and individual image, of which we assume that it is the only mother-image we possess. Yet the powerful primal image still remains in our unconscious, colouring and even determining our individual and conscious life by its influence on our relationship to women, society, our own emotions and our physical nature; this influence, though, works in such subtle ways that we are usually unaware of it.[65]

Jung's assumption is not supported by modern research into infant behaviour, according to which the child experiences 'reality' from the moment of birth; there is no evidence for an archetypal fantasy which gradually gives way to reality as the child grows up. Nevertheless, the longings for 'mother' which can be found in both children and adults, are strikingly similar and can hardly be derived solely from particular, individual mothers. It therefore seems to me that Jung's hypothesis is justified; that there are, in fact, archetypal motherly qualities – both in the sense of a longing for what the 'mother' represents and also in the sense that people are able to develop motherly sides of themselves which do not necessarily derive from their interaction with their own mothers. Mother-images which have little obvious connection with one's own mother also appear in dreams and fantasies. It seems probable that archetypal mother-images are evoked and activated by our relationship to our actual mother. Such mother-images, which are often quite unconscious, exert a powerful influence on our expectations and understanding of the mother role.

In considering archetypal images, we must of course always question to what extent these may be ideological constructs which serve to prop up and cement the status quo; or to what extent they contain – as is implicit in Jung's concept of archetypes[66] – aspects of the psyche which need to be developed, which are as yet 'unredeemed'. Such archetypal images can awaken fantasies which are of use in an individual's inner development. They may even allow us to experience things that have been lacking in our actual life and act as a new, or perhaps strengthened, stimulus to creative impulses. Jung speaks of the creative process as an 'unconscious revitalizing of the archetype, which is developed and delineated in ever greater detail until it appears as a complete work of art'. Further, he says that 'active fashioning of the primal image . . . is in some respects a process of translation into contemporary language and form'.[67] Jung is suggesting – and this too seems to me to require investigation – that those archetypes are always activated which are most lacking in common consciousness. This creative potential – which could only become a real process if the potential was tapped – would appear to allow the psyche to be self-regulating and not only provide the separate individual with experiences necessary to him or her, but also humanity in general with the collective content relevant to particular times and conditions.[68]

Jung often referred to the gods of earlier times, stating that we still encounter them as archetypes in our unconscious.[69] This idea allows us to draw upon the knowledge we have of the gods and goddesses of various mythologies, together with the mysteries and rites connected with them, and apply it to our exploration of the structure of the collective unconscious. By so doing, we can understand more about the themes at work in the depths of the human psyche, which find expression in our fantasies as both memory and expectation.

In recent years there has been an enormous growth of interest in female deities. This alone would suggest that the influence and significance of the feminine has been suppressed for too long. Mother-goddesses are one sub-group of female deities. It seems to me that we can best avoid the danger of defining archetypal motherly qualities in too fixed and rigid a way if, instead of thinking of these mother-goddesses as particular beings, we try to home in on the actual experiences they embody; if we characterize them in the light of the forms they assume in our dreams and fantasies rather than on the basis of the knowledge – to a large degree speculative – that we gain from mythology.

There are many mother-goddesses in mythology. Sometimes it seems that almost all female deities have a mother aspect. This may be partly due to the fact that every female goddess has – at least in theory – the potential to become a mother. But to lay so much emphasis on their motherly character would seem to drastically reduce the multiplicity of their potential. Perhaps it is even as a result of unemancipated mother complexes that goddesses of love are so easily transformed into mother deities. There are very ancient statuettes of the female form which strongly emphasize its sexual characteristics: the breasts and the womb are often depicted as a 'feminine triangle'. Such figures were no doubt part of fertility cults and can be seen as 'very early predecessors of the mother-goddesses'.[70] The potential for bearing children and the ability to nourish them, to give them, in other words, everything that they initially need, was of course of utmost importance for human life and as such was deified. Mother-goddesses are primarily characterized by these attributes of giving birth and nourishment. But we should be clear that there are three distinct aspects to the process of bearing a child: fertile receptivity; carrying to the full term; and pushing out when the time is right.

These characteristics of the goddesses are also transposed onto nature: the earth is seen as a mother who creates and sustains life. A mother-goddess is most closely identified with the earth in mythologies which see her as the partner of a sky-god: she may even be called 'Earth' – as we find, for example, in the Greek term Gaia.

The 'mother of the gods' in Asia Minor was called the Great
Mother. The Greeks also called her Meter Oreia or the Mother
of the Mountain.[71] Stone was the sign and symbol of the mother-
goddess Cybele, whose 'eunuch priests castrated themselves in
honour of the goddess. Connected with her cult was the story of
Attis, whom Meter – the Great Mother – loved; he was castrated
and died under a fir-tree, yet remained the "parhedros" or consort
of the goddess.'[72] She was generally thought of as Mother Earth
and aspects of her worship were projected upon the cultivation of
nature. Castration of priests corresponded to the cutting of corn
for instance; and when her followers wounded themselves in her
honour with swords and knives, this related to the 'wounding' of
the earth at ploughing time.

According to Burkert, the success of the Meter cult was
based upon the 'focus-point of a fixed holy place and its atten-
dant priesthood.'[73] 'About 205 BC, the Romans demanded that
the "Mother" should be transferred to Rome',[74] where there
arose a centre for the cult of Meter. The eunuchs corresponded
no doubt to Attis.

Another well-known mother-goddess was Demeter, whose
name means 'corn-mother' or 'earth-mother'.[75] The myth, with
which we are comparatively familiar,[76] tells that Hades carried
off Persephone, the daughter of Demeter, into the underworld.
Demeter, in anger and sadness, withdrew and allowed no more
corn to grow. Zeus intervened and a bargain was struck in
which Persephone spent one-third of the year in the underworld and the other two-thirds with her mother. Persephone
was seen as an aspect of Demeter, as an underworld goddess;
another aspect of her was Core, the young girl, symbolized by
the green corn-shoots.

In this myth we are struck by the wild, angry grief of Demeter,
by her refusal to take part in life or to speak – until she breaks
into laughter at last and drinks the barley-beer. The main festival
of the Demeter cult was known as Thesmophores and was a
festival for women in which live sucking pigs, snakes and pine-
cones were thrown into the cave of Demeter. This celebration
was intended to aid women's fertility – and by analogy the

fertility of the earth. It was also closely connected with themes of decline and ascent, with death and rebirth in their broadest sense.

This myth can of course be seen as symbolic of the earth's seasonal rhythms, but also of the mysteries of female fertility, which are not simply of a physical nature. All fertility is cyclical and rhythmic; it passes through a phase of decline and inactivity, and then re-emerges in new flowering and fruiting. Death, or a fallow period, is involved in this process. The fact that one of the aspects of the mother-goddess is also the death-goddess must have something to do with this cyclical quality, but also with ideas about death as 'going home' – which one can also easily see as a return to the mother.

Yet another mother-goddess – and perhaps the most archetypal – is the Egyptian Isis, of whom it was said that 'she was present from the beginning, the oldest of the old'. She gave birth to the sun itself.[77] Both gods and mankind were descended from her and nourished by her milk or blood.

The relationship of Isis to Osiris is particularly significant: Osiris is the symbol of the dead god who is miraculously reclaimed from death by Isis. Osiris's brother Seth, his enemy, killed Osiris; his body was strewn and scattered across the ocean. Isis and Nephtys, her dark twin sister, searched everywhere, and Isis found and re-formed the corpse of Osiris, then awoke him with her cries and laments. He then gave her the god Horus – the sun-god with the head of a falcon (which implies that she was originally a sun-goddess herself) – whom she brought up in secret and placed upon the throne of the kingdom. She is often depicted with the boy Horus upon her arm and as such is a forerunner of Mary, the mother of God. Because she had conquered death, she was honoured as one endowed with magic and miraculous powers; later she was thought of as a witch, in which form she aided the sun-god in his battle with the night. In the Graeco-Roman period she was considered a cosmic deity who guided the stars and ruled the waters. Isis and Nephtys were Egyptian versions of the life and death aspects of the mother.

In this connection it is interesting to note that the Sumerian underworld goddess, Ereshkigal, is described as being in labour while dwelling in the realm of death. In this myth, the death-goddess is also the goddess of life.

A central theme in the festivals of Meter, Demeter and Isis must have been the transformation of grief into joy:[78]

> Demeter's grief ends when Persephone returns – the festival in her honour ends with jubilation and the flourishing and swaying of torches; in the 'Mater Magna' (Great Mother) festival, the Dies Sanguinis or Blood-Day is followed by 'Hilaria', the day of happiness; the grief rituals in the cult of Isis end with the discovery of Osiris, embodied in the waters of the Nile, and in the words: 'We have found him, we join together in joy'.[79]

In this interpretation, Isis is seen as the earth, or the 'fertility at work in earth and moon, while Osiris is the fertilizing power of the Nile.'[80] Plutarch extends this significance when he speaks of two contrary forces: 'the good, unifying principle' – represented by Isis who suffers and endows with life – and the principle of fragmentation and destruction – symbolized by Osiris and Seth.

These, then, are the archetypal themes connected with the mother-goddess: the sense of a unifying principle; the transforming of grief into joy – which relates to the experiences of separation and wholeness; the realization that death and life are necessary to, and determine, each other; the biological functions of the mother expressed in terms of bearing, nourishing and letting go; and the symbolic significance of the powers of fertility at work in the earth, which make growth possible and sustain it, but which also withdraw and decline when the time comes.

CHAPTER 6

Aggression and lament

Developing beyond the originally positive mother complex

I have referred continually to an *originally* positive mother complex, which is meant to imply that it does not remain positive unless the ego complex develops in the right way. It must, I believe, be possible to develop beyond this originally positive mother complex in ways which retain its rich abundance, yet also integrate it into adult life. Fairy tales provide us with symbolic examples of such development. They also have the advantage, as opposed to descriptions of psychoanalytical case-histories, that they are short and to the point, and represent common, archetypal processes of psychological development. I will not give any lengthy interpretations of fairy tales here but note only the essential developmental tasks of emancipation from the originally positive mother complex as they are portrayed in two fairy tales: firstly about a hero, and then a heroine.

The Knight with the Shadow of a Laugh

Once, in olden times – and if we had lived then, we would not live now; in those times our story might have been new or not, but we wouldn't have been without one, that's for sure. . . In those days, as I was saying, two people got married. A short time after the wedding the husband died, leaving the wife on her own. Nine months after the wedding, to the very day, she gave birth to a boy. She was lonely and loved the child with all her heart – so much so that she wouldn't have given him away for a heap of gold. For 21 years she kept that child suckling at her breast; and not once in all that time did he leave the house.

So that's how it was, for good or ill. The mother worked herself to the bone for his sake, through the long, hard years. One day he noticed that she had grown old and was turning a little soft in the head. He said to himself that it was high time he took care of his mother and made her comfortable for the rest of her life.

He leapt out of bed, stood in the middle of the floor and stuck his head and shoulders out through the timbers of the roof. And that's how he stayed until his mother came home.

'My darling,' she said, 'you've got out of bed. I hope it agrees with you. Wouldn't you be better off staying in your cradle, instead of looking about like that?'

When he heard his mother's voice, he bent his back and drew his head back into the house. Then he said: 'You've bothered about me too long, mother; I'll work for you from now on.'

'Better late than never, boy of my heart,' she replied.

'Now mother, give me some kind of clothing to dress in, before I go and see other folk.'

So she took bed-linen and fastened it together with thread – not sewed, for she had no needle. The moment he had his skirt on, you couldn't see him for dust. He was off and away and never stopped until he reached a square where a great castle was being built. Scores of men were working at it on all sides. When these workmen saw the tall, scrawny fellow rushing towards them all out of breath and in a pother, every one of them took fright and took to their heels like a flock of hunted sheep.

The widow's son was surprised to see everyone running away. When he got to the castle there was no-one left apart from the foreman; so he asked him for work. The foreman was afraid of him and wouldn't have dared refuse him anything for all the gold in the world. He asked the foreman how much the builders were paid. The man told him. Then the widow's son said: 'If I do the work of twelve men, will you pay me accordingly?'

'Yes,' said the foreman.

'What shall I do first?'

'Over there is a block of stone. Twelve men would lift such a block as high as the four walls. See if you can manage it.'

The widow's son took hold of the block with a sturdy grip and hurled it like a sling-shot.

When the foreman saw this, he put his hand in his pocket and gave him five pounds. He told him to find a shop and buy himself a suit of clothes, and then come back to work. He would pay him the wages of 12 men.

When the widow's son got the money, he didn't wait to be told twice, but ran to the shop. When the shopkeepers caught sight of him, they were scared out of their wits. When he asked for a suit of clothes, they leapt about like wildfire to give him what he wanted. They were so frightened that they forgot to ask him for payment. Long after he'd left, they were still fainting and swooning from terror.

He dressed himself from head to toe. No king's son in all the world looked finer than the widow's son. The sharpest mortal eye could not have recognized him in his new appearance. When he returned to the work-place, the foreman began to bow and defer to him instead of ordering him about. The man thought he was a king's son, come from the East to woo the lovely, gold-cheeked Leamuinn, the daughter of the king whose palace was being built.

So far, so good. To cut a long story short, the widow's son stayed and worked at building the palace until all that was missing were the roof-joists. It hardly needs to be mentioned that he took home to his mother money enough and to spare.

Not long after the castle walls were finished, the king sent forth the following proclamation throughout all the land: whoever dared – be he no more than a poor, naked wretch – to harness the giant snake which was hiding itself away in the depths of the forest, and bring on its back as much wood as was needed for the roof-joists of the castle – that man would win the hand of his daughter, the gold-cheeked Leamuinn; but anyone who undertook this task and failed would be punished with immediate death.

The widow's son was at home at the time and resting. One day he said to his mother: 'Let bad luck and misery be my lot if I don't try my hand at this! I'll not err by a hair's breadth from my aim until I've put my strength to the test and had a go at loading up that great pile of wood on the giant snake's back and riding it back to the castle. Then the king's daughter will be mine.'

'If you listen to my advice,' said his mother, 'you'll have nothing to do with that snake. It's killed scores of people since the time of the Great Flood. I'm afraid for your life if you start messing with it.'

'Mother, I've the strength of a hundred men in the marrow of my bones because you suckled me for twenty-one years. There is nothing on earth that could square up to my strength or make me cower. Farewell, mother. When you see me again, the king's daughter will be your daughter-in-law.'

He hurried away, swift as the March wind – one mile to every step and twelve miles if he put his will to it. He strode through the countryside until he reached the king's palace. He greeted the king and the king returned his greeting.

'I've heard,' he said, 'that the lovely Leamuinn of the golden cheeks will be given in marriage to whoever can do what you require.'

'Yes', said the king. He was amazed at the sight of the widow's son, for never in his life before had he seen such an exquisite man as the one he now beheld.

'I think,' said the king, 'that your limbs and hands are too delicate to be put to such rough work.'

'The topmost point of the roof will show you what I'm made of!' said the widow's son.

'You're a brave young man,' said the king, 'but I think it will not stop your head being stuck on a spear above my great gates, along with all the others that are already there.'

The widow's son did not hang about for long. He was off through the door in a hurry and away to the forest. In the middle of the forest lay a wide lake in which dwelt the giant snake. It came only rarely to the shore; but when it did, it devoured as much as would keep it from hunger and hunting for a week.

Cathal – for that was the name of the widow's son – strode through the forest. He looked sharply this way and that. It was not long before he found the snake's slimy trail on the grass. He followed it until he saw the snake in the far distance, apparently asleep.

He grasped an elm, tore it out by the roots and split the lower four feet of it open. He also pulled an ash-tree out of the ground and carried it in his hand like a walking stick. Then he crept quickly and quietly behind the great worm's tail, clamped the last two feet of its length between the split end of the elm-trunk and banged a wedge through tree and tail. The moment the wedge was driven through its tail, the snake leapt into the air and lifted Cathal high over the forest. He took a firm hold on the crown of the tree and, using all his strength, brought the monster to earth. It didn't have much luck. As it plummeted to the ground, it turned and tried to pull Cathal towards itself. But he lifted the ash and struck the snake such a blow below the ears that it was dead to the world for the next five hours.

Next Cathal began to pull up trees by the roots and throw them upon the snake's back. When he thought he had enough wood for the palace, he struck the snake again behind its left ear, which made it squeal. But he kept striking it, blow upon blow, and drove it before him until he came to the king's cattle-pen.

The king's men were watching from the highest window of the castle. When they saw Cathal and the mountain of wood slithering before him towards them, they thought him the world's greatest magician. They couldn't believe their eyes. They didn't believe that there could be a man anywhere on earth who could harness the snake as he had done.

After Cathal had driven the snake and its load up to the castle, he left it there and stepped towards the great gates. The king came out to meet him. 'You've a good strong set of bones!' the king said to him. 'You are the bravest hero in all the world.'

'Thank you,' replied Cathal, 'and I think I have earned your daughter, have I not?'

'I am perfectly happy to give her to you,' said the king. 'However you must first go and see her yourself.'

'That's fine by me,' answered Cathal.

The king led him in to meet Leamuinn. She said: 'I am not yours yet – you have won only a third of me. You must still take the snake back to the wood and kill it. When you've done that you must travel to the East and return in one year to the day, to tell me why it is that the knight with the shadow of a laugh has not laughed for seven years. You must also bring me word of the death of the dreadful hag with icy teeth. When you have done all that, then I'll agree to be your wife. But be warned: if these things are not done before the time is up, I'll make dust and ashes of your bones!'

'Oh, that's all grist to my mill,' said Cathal, and away he went.

In a moment or two, he'd unloaded the wood from the snake's back. Then he took his ash-stick and gave the snake a powerful blow behind the ears. Before much longer had passed, they were both back in the middle of the forest. Then Cathal began to strike the snake with the thick end of the tree, so that it soon stopped waggling its ears and never stirred again. Cathal then drew a knife from his belt and cut out the tip of its tongue – just in case others should pass that way and tell the king's daughter that they had killed the snake.

He never looked back but headed for the coast. There he found a boat on the shore and going aboard began to steer it out – the prow towards the ocean, the stern towards the land. He unfurled its colourful sails, both large and small, and hauled them to the top of the mast. The boat was powered one-third by oars and two-thirds by sails. It ploughed through the ocean, climbing one moment so high it nearly turned a somersault, the next moment plunging down and filling up to the brim with water. It sped along in a whirl of white foam and a flurry of grey sand whisked up from the bottom. In front of Cathal the sea lay blue-green, behind him it was red as blood. The soughing of the sails and the roaring of the waves were pleasant sounds in his ears. His oar-strokes sounded to him like all the song-birds of the East.

Whether it took him a long or a short time, he arrived on Eastern shores; and so great was the speed of his travelling that he glided on far over the land, fetching up at a place where there was no danger of being burnt by the sun or whipped by storms. A leafy bush gave him shelter.

Cathal rested, then stood up. His limbs were rather stiff. His bones were like a little child's. But he walked about and they soon stretched and loosened up. He went on his way. Often his body felt feeble and weak. He began to think how alone he was in this strange land, without a friend or help of any kind, and of how time was pressing. His cheerfulness sank like a stone as he realized that he was without mother or wife or house or home. Yet he pulled himself together and wandered on. There was, at any rate, nothing he met that made him the least bit afraid.

After a few days he suddenly found himself by a great cattle-pen, in a place where there were numerous buildings. On their walls grew grey moss, for no-one looked after them. After wandering about for a while, he saw a door in the side-wall of one of the houses. It was so low that he had difficulty in getting in, even on all fours. Once inside he saw in front of him the door of a room. There stood an ancient old woman. Her face was etched with the lines of worry and care. She went quickly into the room and Cathal heard from within the sound of two people talking. Then he stepped forwards and encountered the old woman in the doorway.

'Is this your farm?' he asked. 'Or does someone of better quality live here?'

'It does not belong to me,' she replied, 'but to a man who is better than you are. And you're bold and ill-mannered to walk in just like that and start asking about the owner.'

'Tell me the name of the man who lives here,' said Cathal.

She did not deign to reply. Then, with one long step, he was inside the door. Looking around he saw a slender, tall man with an expressionless face who was lying on his back on the bed.

Before Cathal had time to say a word of greeting, the man leapt from the bed and grabbed him by the throat. There was a good deal of shoving and wrestling. The fight those two enormous fellows fought had never before seen its like in all the world. In the middle of it, Cathal was suddenly struck by the fact that he had no-one close at hand to take his part; he thought of his mother, left alone at home, and was seized by furious despair. With his utmost strength he gave the man from the bed a great push which sent him flying into the fire. Feeling the heat of the flames, the man cried out and begged Cathal to let him free and to heal his burning blisters, and then he would do whatever Cathal required.

'Before you get out of the fire, tell me your name, or I'll drive the life out of you to the very last drop!'

'I am the knight with the shadow of a laugh, and I have not laughed for seven years.'

'You are the one,' said the widow's son, 'whom I've been seeking all this time!'

Saying this, he lifted the knight with both hands, placed him on the edge of the bed and rubbed spittle into his burning wounds, and in an instant he was as well and whole again as he had been before the fight.

They both sat and watched each other for a while, like the cat watching the mouse. After a little, the widow's son heard a woman shrieking in a loud voice behind the walls. It sounded to him like air and earth crashing and clashing together, so terrible were her cries. He gave the knight a sideways glance and saw from the contorted expression on his face that he had no liking either for these screams. Suddenly the knight asked the widow's son: 'Whose son are you? Or where do you come from?'

'I am the son of a great champion from Ireland; I undertook this adventure to find out about you and to learn why it is that you have not laughed for these seven years.'

'I have no desire to tell you just at the moment. But maybe I'll tell you the reason some other time.'

The knight clapped his hands and the old woman appeared.

'Have you prepared the evening meal?' he asked her.

'Yes,' she said.

'Bring it to us here!'

Soon there stood a fine, tasty meal before them. Every bite tasted of honey and no two bites tasted the same. When they had eaten and drunk their fill, they went to bed.

Cathal lay down, but his thoughts kept returning to that wild shrieking he had heard earlier in the evening. He decided to leave no stone unturned until he had satisfied his curiosity – without anyone noticing what he was up to – and found out whose throat the screams had come from.

Next morning he got up, washed his face and walked around a bit, without eating anything first. After he had wandered about for an hour or so, he spied something far off in the distance. When he got nearer he saw it was a horse. When he was within a stone's throw of it, he saw it was mouse-grey. It heard the noise of his feet, lifted up its head and whinnied when it saw him. Straight away another horse came galloping over the field and both horses took to their heels and fled as swift as the March wind. Cathal followed them as fast as he could, keeping them in his sights the whole time. At last and at length, when he'd blown his soul to the four winds with the effort of running, he saw the horses heading for a round clearing in the forest. He followed them and came to a horse-pen. Just as he was bending low to squeeze through under its cross-beams, one of the animals neighed. He didn't have long to wait. A great, old woman came towards him with froth on her mouth. The moment he set eyes on her he was so terrified that his soul nearly sank into his boots. As she drew closer to him she said:

'By the beard I'll grab you quick
And stretch your neck my little chick;
I've a nose for such a one,
You false, you thieving Irishman.'

'I'm not a false, thieving Irishman,' said Cathal, 'but a true champion.'

'What would you like best?' she asked. 'To fight with me on blood-red stones until I suck out your bones like soup? Or shall I hack your ribs to pieces with a thrice-sharpened knife, and cut your flesh and skin to ribbons while your blood washes the ground? No bird will ever find the smallest bone of you, for I'll mix your corpse with earth and strew it around in a seven-mile ring.'

'I'd rather fight you on reddened stones,' said the widow's son. 'My strength will flatten you into the ground, so that no bird will even get a taste of your flesh nor a smell of your bones.'

'You're too much for one bite, but too little for two,' said the hag. 'If I had a grain of salt to season you I'd take you between my long, hungry teeth.'

Cathal gave no hint of weakness in danger. He grabbed her. Such fighting and fraying had never been seen before anywhere in the world, neither in the West nor in the East. The stones on top of the ground were pushed under, and those underneath were pushed up. Their fighting made soft what had been hard, and springs of water shot up out of grey stones.

Near the end of the day, the widow's son felt exhausted. The thought came to him that he had no-one to mourn him or lay him out nicely for burial. At this, he grasped the old hag by her sides with all his strength. But she was so strong that this did not shake her. The sun went down behind the hill; Cathal grew weak and the hag had a joyous glimpse of victory over this fine knight. But before his strength had quite deserted him, a wren flew down and landed upon the tip of the old witch's nose and stuck its beak into her eyes. At that, she became suddenly as weak as a goose.

She sank down before him like a sheaf of straw and he bent to the ground and struck the vein in her neck, so that she stopped stirring and her ears, too, never waggled again. Once he had laid her low, he drew the knife from his belt and cut off the tip of her tongue. Then he rushed into the witch's palace and ransacked it from top to bottom. Every room in the house was full of gold or silver, but he saw no other human being. Then he returned to the horse-pen, tied the horses to the manger and hurried back to the knight's house. He said nothing of what had befallen him.

Just as on the previous evening, the knight offered him a good supper. After eating, they settled down and conversed a little. Night came; and as the hag's shrieking had not been heard, the knight was astonished. He believed, since he himself had been unable to defeat her, that no-one else in the world would have the power to do so.

Then Cathal said: 'I do not hear the shrieking as I did last night. And I think I will never hear it again!' The knight smiled and replied: 'That old witch has been living here as long as people can remember. The island was in her power; she ravaged, plagued and burnt every nook and cranny of it, so that no-one lives here any more except me and the old woman who serves me. Many times I fought with the witch, but in the end I gave up all hope and had no stomach for further battles with her. Not one night has passed in these last seven years, since misfortune and misery befell me, in which she has not let out her shriek in the dead hour of the night so that my affliction should have no end.'

'But now tell me why you have the shadow of a laugh,' said Cathal. 'You may rest assured that you will never hear the old hag's voice again as long as you live.'

The knight began to relate the cause of his distress, and said: 'Tomorrow it will be exactly seven years since I ruled here over a great kingdom. I sent an invitation to the noblest of the land, asking them to come to a celebration. I had a fine, comfortable, warm house; and 24 horses stood ready for the hunt each day before my door. The table was laid for the feast; I myself sat at the head of the table and began to carve the meat. Then I looked up and saw through the window the hare with evil breath rolling about in the pond below the horse-pen. He crawled out of the pond, ran up to the linen spread out on the other side of the house, and threw himself into the middle of it so that not an inch of it was not muddied and befouled. Then he dashed up towards us, right up to the window-sill. The day was close and hot and so the window was open. The hare stretched his neck out and breathed into the room, spoiling all the food.'

'I called to my servants and ordered them to saddle the horses and loose the dogs. I myself took my grey stallion and we all stormed off after the hare. Sometimes the dogs' snouts came within a hair's breadth of the hare's tail, but in the next instant he was a mile ahead of us again. In this way he mocked us the whole day long. I kept driving the dogs and urging my men to follow the hare and catch it. This went on for a long time, until at last we pursued the animal into a deep valley that lay between two hills. As the last of my followers entered the valley, it opened and swallowed us up – dogs, servants, horses and all. Suddenly we found ourselves facing 24 robbers and their leader. They began to mock me and my men. One of them took a broom and swept all the dirt that was there into the mouths of my men. The leader said: 'There's plenty of meat here if you can cook it for your entourage.' He had a great iron spit upon which was stuck a wild boar, and told me to take it and turn it over the fire for my men. I took hold of the spit as he ordered. In those days I was no mean champion. But I could sooner have cut myself in four pieces than have lifted the boar from the ground. Then the leader asked me what kind of heroic deeds we did back home apart from stuffing ourselves with food. Before I could think of a suitable reply, he threw a great block of iron into the middle of the fire. Through the middle of the block went a chain. When the block was red-hot, the robber-chief and his men drew it out of the fire. His men stood on one side, my men on the other, and they all had to grasp hold of the chain that passed through the middle of the block and pull upon it in a tug-of-war against each other. But the robbers proved stronger and hauled on the chain so that my men were all pulled up to the block until nothing remained of them, for their bodies melted in the raging heat. I stood and watched, wondering whether my turn would be next.'

After they had dealt with my followers in this way, one of the robbers came with a magic wand and struck my servants, horses and dogs, turning them instantly to a pile of stones. He wanted to do the same to me. But the robber-chief would not allow it, saying that I was clearly the leader of my band, and gave me permission to return home. He opened a door and let me out, and it took me a good year to take the same way back that we had covered in one day on the wild hare chase.'

Once home, I threw myself upon my bed and refused to rise again, nor did I laugh from that day until this. The robber band put a spell on my palace and everything that was mine, apart from myself and the old woman who served me. And since this misery came upon me, no-one has been able to overcome the dreadful hag, who has shrieked in my ears all through the seven years. During this time she has ransacked and burnt the whole island and destroyed all who once lived here.'

'Until the day of judgement comes she will never kill anyone again!' said Cathal. 'You had good reason to be sad and afflicted and not to laugh for seven years! Now I thank you for telling me the reason for the shadow of your laugh. Don't worry yourself any more about the old hag, for I tell you now that I have killed her.'

'I believed,' said the knight, 'that no-one on earth was capable of breaking her back. I was secretly planning to fight with you, but since you have killed the destroyer of this land, I have nothing more against you.'

After eating their evening meal they went to sleep. Cathal slept softly and well until the next morning; and the moment dawn broke he was up and about, getting himself ready to go to the old hag's palace, which he intended to put under lock and key to keep it safe for Leamuinn when she came, so as to live there with her.

When he thought it was time to eat, he went to the knight. And, indeed, a tasty meal was laid before him. But Cathal lifted his head and, looking out of the window, saw something about the size of a dog. It was running in and out of the horse-pen. Cathal made a sign to the knight to look. The knight looked up and recognized the hare with the evil breath, that had last come seven years ago.

'Bad luck and misery!' he cried. 'If only we had horses we would give the hare a good chase once more.'

'Come with me,' said Cathal, 'and we'll soon have a pair of horses better than any man has ever ridden before.'

The knight followed Cathal and they hurried along the path which led to the old hag's palace, until they came to the horse-pen. The widow's son took hold of one of the horses and told the knight to mount the other. He did what he was told and was whisked away, followed by Cathal. They kept a true course and the hare led them the same way that he had led the knight seven years ago.

When they arrived in the robbers' den, the robbers laughed at them in mockery. Cathal said: 'What are you laughing at?' He took a broom and swept all the dirt that had gathered in seven years into their mouths. Then he took hold of the wild boar as easily as a bundle of straw and cooked it for no more than a couple of minutes. Then he gave the knight meat from it to eat. Next he took the iron block, threw it into the fire and, when it was red-hot, drew it once more from the fire. He stood on one side of the block and the robbers on the other side. But as hard as the robbers pulled on the chain, Cathal pulled harder, until every one of them was melted to a lump of fat. Then Cathal took hold of the robber-chief and was about to treat him in the same way. But the knight called out to him that he should spare the man, for he had allowed him to leave the den unharmed. 'And,' he continued, 'if you return the servants, horses and dogs that came here with me seven years ago, we will leave you undisturbed.'

The robber chief was terrified that he might be killed. Since he could see that Cathal had the strength of hundreds, he thought it best to reawaken to life and strength all that he had once taken from the knight. He accomplished this as quickly as he could. He struck the stone pile three times with the magic wand; and, in less time than it takes to turn around, men, dogs and horses were once more as alive as they had ever been. Cathal ordered the robber to open the door quickly. This was done and the whole troop stormed off.

They were soon back home, and the knight saw as he drew near that everything was once more as it had been – his castle, farms, all that belonged to him, were as lovely as they had been before the hare with the evil breath had come to spoil things. His heart was bursting with joy that the old witch was dead. He and his attendants had the suppleness of their limbs again. He settled back into his house and castle; but he was sorry that he could not hold a feast for the people of the kingdom, for there were none left on the island other than those in his immediate circle. The old witch had destroyed everything.

He had no thought at all of killing Cathal, as he had originally planned when Cathal first appeared; instead he offered him half of all he owned. Cathal would accept nothing for he knew he was richer. With many blessings and good wishes on both sides, Cathal took his departure, saying that if he should have the good luck to remain alive he would not fail to come back and visit the knight. In joyful mood he soon arrived home.

When he entered the palace of Leamuinn's father, everyone welcomed him. They all thought he had fallen between millstones and come to a sticky end.

But someone else was there before him, a knight whom Leamuinn had also sent on his travels, and who had returned already with the skulls of the old hag and the snake. This man was thought to be the greatest hero on earth. He had told them that Cathal had been killed; and so his marriage to Leamuinn was now being celebrated. This was the very moment when the widow's son appeared on the scene. But, since he had not brought his opponents' heads, Leamuinn didn't believe a word of what he said.

'I cut off their heads,' said Cathal, 'and after I'd done that, I cut their tongue-tips off. And the proof of the pudding is in the eating. So here are the tongue-tips I cut off after I'd conquered the snake and the witch!'

The king took a good look into the jaws of the two heads and saw that the tongue-tips were missing. Immediately he announced: 'Cathal did these heroic deeds!' Thereupon Cathal told the king's daughter of the knight with the shadow of a laugh and of all that had happened on his travels, and everyone believed him. Leamuinn put her two arms around his neck and drew him to her heart.

> She pressed him with kisses,
> Wet him with her tears,
> Dried him with soft silk
> And satin cloths.

When the other knight saw that he was poorly esteemed, he got hot under the collar and spoke rudely to the king. The widow's son stretched out his fist and gave him a blow beneath the chin, at which he was laid out flat and never spoke another word.

To make a long story short: a marriage was celebrated to which all were invited, even the poor and naked. After the wedding the widow's son took his wife and his mother to live in the old hag's palace. Her gold and silver and all her treasures belonged to them and their children and their childrens' children.

In time, they went the way of all wood, while I came by a better way. They died, while I kept myself out of the coffin. And if these are lies, why, the dog can carry them off in his jaws.[81]

This folktale begins with a description of an originally positive mother complex that has been retained far longer than normal. The fact that the father died shortly after the wedding has allowed this mother complex to survive in an extreme form. 'She was lonely and loved the child with all her heart . . . ' For 21 years she suckles him at her breast. This statement, metaphorical though it is, tells us a great deal. It is common for a parent's loneliness to hinder a child from developing independence. At the age of 21, Cathal notices that his mother 'had grown old and was turning a little soft in the head'. He decides that it is now time to care for his mother; he gets out of bed, rather against the will of his mother, whose power to control him and confine him within his 'cradle' has now grown weaker. He is driven from his bed, though, by sympathy for his mother. Sympathy and a readiness to help are symptomatic of an originally positive mother complex.

He seeks work at the castle and is immediately able to assess his own capacity and strength: he can do the work of 12 men and wishes to be paid accordingly. He works at building the walls of the castle – symbolic of a clear and secure distinction between inner and outer worlds; he is creating the boundaries of his ego complex, marking out his own inner space. The protection and narrow boundaries of his mother's cradle are expanded to become a castle, for which a roof must be made.

Wood for it must be transported on the back of the giant snake, which has hidden itself in the forest. Whoever can manage this will win the hand of the king's daughter. Cathal is ready to attempt this now that he has shown an ability to get to grips with life, to command respect and to support both himself and his mother – all expressions of an active and responsible ego capacity. But still more is needed: he must form a connection and relationship with a woman of his own age. This means, symbolically, that he needs to find access to his anima, to the mysterious and alluring inner female aspect of himself, which will allow him to overcome the exclusive love for his mother. His mother is not best pleased by his plans! She warns him of the giant snake's potential for destruction, but he reassures her and flatters her self-esteem by saying that he has the strength of a hundred men because she suckled him so long. Nothing, he says, can frighten him. His strength, incidentally, has increased

– previously he had the power of 12 men. He is continually described as a handsome, even exquisite man. He is strong and confident. This is one consequence of the excess of motherly nourishment that he has received. He feels in full possession of his powers, convinced that he can overcome any difficulty or task which presents itself. But now he must prove himself. The tasks which confront him are all developmental needs from which he was protected in the mother–son relationship. Harnessing and then killing the giant snake, finding out why the knight with the shadow of a laugh has not laughed for seven years, bringing proof of the death of the dreadful hag with the icy teeth – these are all hidden aspects of his personality, the shadow side of the excessive spoiling and protection he received from his mother. Either he must come to terms with these things, or, in the language of the folktale, he will die.

What is the more precise significance of each of the stages he passes through? The snake which devours everything available, so that it does not need to hunt again for a week, could be interpreted as a devouring tendency towards regression, towards laziness, which Cathal succeeds in discovering in himself and then disarming and putting to his service through aggression. He defends himself with almost manic strength against the danger of passivity and indolence, which would otherwise lead him to make only sporadic and greedy excursions into the outer world, to take what he needs. The snake represents the shadow aspect of his nourishing mother complex: a devouring, lazy, greedy tendency which he harnesses and destroys in order to win the king's daughter. People with an originally positive mother complex usually only reject such regressive tendencies if they are likely, as a result, to radically improve the quality and intensity of their life. They have enough energy for this task, but they will seldom apply it unless they experience the pernicious quality of their regressive tendencies, which express themselves in pipe-dreams that are never close enough to real emotions to be made proper use of. Once they gain insight into the negative effects of their regression, they can mobilize the enormous forces which are at their disposal.

Cathal may believe that once the snake has been harnessed he has achieved all that was needed. The king's daughter, however, knows better. She is aware that he will not be ready for a relationship with her until he has tackled some further problems that still reside in his unconscious. So, undismayed by her further demands, he sets sail for the East. Again we sense the energy that is available to him; but only one-third of the power which propels him comes directly from his own efforts, from his 'oar-strokes'. The other two-thirds are given him by the wind and the elements, which expresses his close and sustaining relationship with the forces of nature. There is also, though, another, less comfortable aspect of the force of the elements. Behind him the sea appears blood-red; and soon after, he is troubled by feelings of rootlessness and loneliness. These descriptions indicate that he has begun to touch into a realm within himself that is uncertain and forlorn – which is typical for the originally positive mother complex when the world no longer appears in the guise of an all-giving mother, or at least when there is no possibility of speedy gratification or reward for some great achievement, such as conquering the giant snake.

Cathal's experience of despondency is embodied in the image of buildings overgrown by thick moss, which have no doubt been uninhabited for a very long time. At last he gains access to this forgotten, or bewitched, complex of buildings and finds an old woman with a sad and anxious face and 'a slender, tall man with an expressionless face who was lying on his back on the bed'. Cathal and he engage in a tremendous fight, until the fire's fierce heat makes the knight promise to do whatever Cathal requires.

This shows us that Cathal is still struggling with his alter ego, with the aspect of himself which cannot lift itself, metaphorically, out of bed. It is typical of the originally positive mother complex that Cathal is not suffering from a lack of strength, but from an absence of motherly support. Simply thinking of his mother is enough to mobilize the forces of despair which he needs to survive and develop.

The knight, the shadow-side of Cathal's identity, must now name himself as the one 'with the shadow of a laugh' whom Cathal has been seeking. The knight is cured of his blisters by Cathal's healing spittle. Soon afterwards comes 'a woman shrieking in a loud voice. . . It sounded to him like air and earth crashing and clashing together. . . ' The knight's suffering becomes more and more pronounced. At this point in the story we can sense that we are approaching its high-point, and also the nub of the unconscious disturbance and difficulty. This is accentuated by the fact that all four elements come together in one passage. Air – frequently associated with the male principle; and earth – the female – clash together, suggesting how difficult it is for Cathal to unite the two principles within himself.

Cathal meets an old hag frothing at the mouth, a figure who fills him with dread. She is a destroyer, but nevertheless still offers him the choice of fighting with her or being killed without resistance. They fight more fiercely than has ever been fought before: 'Their fighting made soft what had been hard, and springs of water shot up out of grey stones.' This image expresses in a peculiarly apt way Cathal's battle with the personification of destruction and greed. He is nearly overcome by it, but the struggle itself opens new 'springs', new sources of insight for him. Towards evening he comes to the end of his strength, which is only renewed by the thought that he is alone, that there is no-one to mourn him. But this despairing strength is also not sufficient. At the very point when the hag senses victory, a wren lands upon her nose and pecks at her eyes, so that she grows weak and Cathal can kill her. A lucky chance perhaps, as expressed in an optimistic phrase frequently used by those with an originally positive mother complex: 'Things will sort themselves out somehow.' But it is also true that Cathal has done everything in his power to defeat the old hag, and then unexpected help comes to him from beyond himself. Or at least a different, delicate kind of strength comes to him, more like a shift in perception, so that he is no longer enmeshed in a witch-like, destructive way of seeing.

The knight 'with the shadow of a laugh' had fought in vain with the hag. She was not able to kill him, but he had not laughed for seven years, dominated by her destructive, life-negating power, which had devastated the surrounding area. His desolation may well symbolize self-destructive tendencies which spoil and undermine the basis of his own well-being and which have until now proved stronger than his capacity for self-determination.

But that is not all: when we laugh, we express our pleasure. The knight's laughter is overshadowed by a threatening undertone of anger and pain – to such an extent that he has suppressed it altogether for seven years. He tells his story. He had enjoyed a rich abundance of life on the island. There had been other people living there with whom he was happily connected, until the 'hare with evil breath' tempted him and his followers into a valley which swallowed them all up.

But Cathal can now reassure the knight. He has killed the old hag and is able to perform all the tasks which the knight previously failed in.

The hare is an animal known for its nervous and panicky disposition. It also embodies the principle of fertility and in ancient times was sacrificed to Aphrodite. It is, too, the animal of Artemis, who was known as the archetypal mother of all witches;[82] this all suggests that a self-assured, sensual form of femininity was feared and, as such, castigated as witch-like. At any rate there is a connection between the fear-inducing hare, the witch and the robber band – which 'put a spell on my palace and everything that was mine . . . ' The hare could represent the anxiety that is activated when people remain enmeshed too long in an originally positive mother complex.

The robbers dwell in the same region – inhabit therefore the same 'complex-realm'. The horses on which Cathal and the knight chase after the 'hare with evil breath' once belonged to the witch; they show the unbridled vitality that was repressed by the destructiveness she represents, which is then released at her death. On them the hare can easily be followed. The robber band symbolizes the forces of male aggression, which have a tendency to demoralize other men, to rob them of their strength and courage by making a mockery of them. This is the main function of the robbers in this story: they prove to the knight, above all, that he is inadequate as a man.

The man with an originally positive mother complex will be confronted by doubt as to whether he is a 'real man'. If his mother assures him that he is, this is of no value; if someone else assures him of it, it is equally of no value, since it does not come from his mother! A man with this form of complex needs to experience – usually in a friendship with another man in which rivalry has been set aside, and in which both pursue a common aim – that he can assert himself against men who try to demoralize him, is equal to them and is able to stand up for himself.

This robber band had turned against the knight with the shadow of a laugh and condemned him to take to his bed: in other words, to be laid low by a depressive form of regression and continually recurring feelings of guilt.

Through aggressive persistence, Cathal and the knight with the shadow of a laugh together overcome these thieving, demoralizing, destructive forces. By becoming aware of the power contained in the originally positive mother complex, Cathal is able to perceive its shadow-side – the troubled, depressive, overwhelmed part of himself, which has difficulty in relating to others. Only then can he deal with the destructive aspects of the complex, which desperately need to be dealt with. That Cathal succeeds in all his undertakings with such apparent ease can lead us to overlook the fact that his life is at stake. If he should fail, death awaits him.

It is interesting that, when he finally wins the hand of the king's daughter, he moves with his new wife and mother into the castle of the old witch whom he has killed. Her treasures now belong to him. Once the destructive aspect of the mother complex has been overcome, all the riches inherent in it become available; it is then possible to form a loving relationship with a woman, and also a friendly relationship with the mother. We should notice as well that the complex is not simply projected onto the mother herself. Cathal only really begins to confront and come to terms with it when his mother is distinguished from the effects of the mother complex, which are personified and embodied in hare, hag and robber band.[83]

The Goose-girl

A folk-tale illustrating female development

Since the originally positive mother complex encroaches less on a woman's search for identity than it does on a man's, the processes of emancipation as illustrated in folktales are also less dramatic. I will use the well-known story *The Goose-Girl* to shed light on the main themes and phases of female emancipation from the originally positive mother complex.

There was once a queen who had grown old. Her husband had long since died, but she had a lovely daughter. The princess was growing up and so was promised in marriage to a king's son who lived far away. The time came at last for the wedding to take place and for the child to undertake her journey to the distant kingdom. Her old mother therefore packed for her a fine trousseau of exquisite treasures: gold and silver, jewelled cups, trinkets and precious things – in fact everything which belonged to a royal dowry, for she loved her child with all her heart. She also gave her a maid-servant to ride with her, who was to hand her over to the bridegroom. Each of them had a horse for the journey, but the horse of the king's daughter was called Falada and could speak. When the time had come for farewells, the old mother went into her bedroom, took a small knife and cut her fingers with it so that they bled, then caught three drops of her blood upon a handkerchief. This she gave to her daughter, saying: 'My dearest child, keep this carefully, for you will have need of it on your journey.'

The two then took sorrowful leave of each other. The princess tucked the handkerchief into her bosom, close to her heart, mounted her horse and set off to find her betrothed. After riding for an hour or so, she felt very thirsty and called to her maidservant: 'Dismount and fetch me water from the stream in my cup which is in your keeping, for I wish to drink.' 'If you are thirsty,' said the maidservant, 'get down and drink from the water yourself – I don't wish to be your serving-maid!' The king's daughter was so thirsty that she got down from her horse, bent down to the water's edge and drank – though not from her golden cup. Then she spoke under her breath: 'Ah Heavens!' And the three drops of blood answered: 'If this your mother knew, her heart would break in two.' But the king's daughter was humble, said nothing and mounted her horse once more.

They continued to ride for a good few miles; the day was hot, the sun scorching, and soon she felt thirsty again. Just then they passed a waterfall and she called out once more to her maidservant: 'Dismount and give me water to drink in my golden cup!' She had already forgotten the maid's unkind words. But the maid now answered still more haughtily: 'Drink if you want to – help yourself. I've no wish to serve you.' The king's daughter was so thirsty that she got down again, bent weeping to the flowing water and said: 'Ah Heavens!' Then the drops of blood answered once more: 'If this your mother knew, her heart would break in two.' And as she was leaning far over and drinking, the handkerchief with the three blood-drops fell from her bosom and floated away on the water; and because she was so troubled she did not notice. But the maidservant noticed and now rejoiced that she would have power over the bride – for by losing the drops of blood she had become weak. When the princess was about to mount her horse Falada again, the maidservant said: 'It will be more fitting for me to ride upon Falada – you can ride my old nag.' The maidservant also ordered her to take off her rich clothes and hand them over, and put on her own shabby ones instead; and to swear by the wide heavens above that she would say nothing about it to anyone when they arrived at the court of the prince. If she had not sworn she would have been killed on the spot. But Falada saw and remembered everything that passed.

The maidservant mounted now upon Falada while the true bride climbed upon the old nag. On they went until at last they arrived at the royal castle. There was great joy at their coming; the king's son rushed to meet them, lifted the maidservant from her steed, thinking that she was his bride, and led her up the palace stairs; while the true king's daughter had to wait below. The old king happened to look out of the window and see her. He noticed that she was very delicate and beautiful. He went into the royal chamber and asked his son's bride who the person was who had accompanied her, who was now standing below in the courtyard. 'Oh her, I just brought her along for company. Give her some work so that she doesn't stand idle.' But the old king could think of no work for her. At last he said: 'I have a young fellow who looks after the geese; she can help him.' The boy was called little Conrad; and from then on the true bride had to help him look after the geese.

Soon though, the false bride said to the young king: 'Dearest husband, please do me a little favour!' He replied: 'Of course I will, gladly.' 'In that case, call the knacker's man and have him slit the throat of the horse upon which I rode. It was a nuisance on the way here.' In fact she was afraid that the horse would reveal how she had behaved to the king's daughter. But before this deed was done, the real princess heard about it. Then she went to the knacker and secretly promised him a piece of gold in return for doing her a small favour. In the town there was a great, dark doorway which she had to pass through morning and evening with the geese. She begged him to nail up Falada's head to the gate so that she could see him again as before. The knacker's man promised, then cut off the horse's head and nailed it to the dark doorway.

In the early morning as she and little Conrad drove out the geese through the gateway, she spoke as she passed: 'Alas, Falada, hanging there.' And the head replied:

'Alas young queen who passes here,
If this your mother knew,
Her heart would break in two.'

On they went out of the town, driving the geese into the open fields. When they reached the meadows, she sat down and unbound her hair; it was pure silver, and when little Conrad saw it he was delighted how it shone and wanted to pull out a few strands. Then she said:

'Now blow you little winds I say,
Blow little Conrad's hat away
And float it here, there, everywhere
For him to chase; until my hair
Is braided and bound for another day.'

Then such a strong wind came blowing that it lifted little Conrad's hat from his head and blew it away over hill and dale so that he had to run after it. When he returned, she'd finishd all her combing and braiding and he couldn't snatch a single strand. He was cross and refused to speak to her. They looked after the geese until evening, then made their way back.

The next morning, when they were going out through the dark gateway, the maiden said: 'Alas, Falada, hanging there.' And the head replied:

'Alas young queen who passes here,
If this your mother knew,
Her heart would break in two.'

When they reached the meadows she sat down once more and began to comb out her hair. Little Conrad ran up to snatch at it but she quickly spoke these words:

'Now blow you little winds I say,
Blow little Conrad's hat away

And float it here, there, everywhere
For him to chase; until my hair
Is braided and bound for another day.'

Then the wind blew, lifting the hat from his head so that it sailed off into the distance and he had to run after it. When he returned, she had long since finished plaiting her hair. He couldn't catch hold of a single strand. They looked after the geese again until evening.

But in the evening, when they came home, little Conrad went to the old king and said: 'I won't look after geese with that girl any more.' 'Why not?' asked the king. 'She annoys me all day long,' he replied. The old king commanded him to say more. Little Conrad replied: 'Every morning when we go out with the geese through the dark doorway, she says to a nag's head that's nailed up: 'Alas, Falada, hanging there.' Then the head replies:

'Alas young queen who passes here,
If this your mother knew,
Her heart would break in two.'

Little Conrad continued, telling the king all that passed in the meadows, and how he had to chase after his hat which the wind blew away.

But the old king commanded him to go with her again the following day. In the early morning, he himself went to the dark doorway and hid himself behind it; then he heard how the maiden spoke with the head of Falada. He also followed her out into the meadows; and, hiding himself in a bush, saw with his own eyes how the goose-girl and the goose-boy brought the flock to the fields, and how, after a while, she sat down and brushed out her hair which shone with radiance, then said:

'Now blow you little winds I say,
Blow little Conrad's hat away
And float it here, there, everywhere
For him to chase; until my hair
Is braided and bound for another day.'

The wind came blowing and little Conrad's hat went sailing away so that he had to run after it while the maiden quietly continued to comb and braid her hair. The king saw it all. Then, unnoticed, he made his way back. In the evening, when the goose-girl came home, he called her to him and asked her why she did all these things. 'I may not tell you nor anyone,' she answered, 'for I swore an oath under the wide heavens that I would not; and had I not sworn, I should have lost my life.' But he insisted and would not leave her in peace. At last he said: 'If you will not tell me, why not at least tell the chimney-stove?' 'Yes,' she said, 'that I will do.' So she crept into the great stove and poured out her heart, telling of all that had befallen and how she had been betrayed by the wicked maidservant. But there was a hole in the tiles of the stove; the old king eavesdropped and heard every word.

Then all was well: she was soon dressed in royal clothes and everyone marvelled at her beauty. The old king called his son and showed him that he had married the false bride who was just a maidservant; and that the maiden who now stood before him, who had been the goose-girl, was the true bride. The young king was glad at heart when he perceived her beauty and goodness, and a great feast was made ready to which all good friends were invited. At the head of the table sat the bridegroom, with the king's daughter on one side of him and the maidservant on the other; but the maidservant was dazzled and blinded and did not recognize the princess in her shining clothes.

After they had eaten and drunk and were merry, the old king turned to the maidservant and set her a riddle: what punishment, he asked, would a lady deserve who had betrayed someone else in such and such a manner – and he described all that had happened. Then the false bride said: 'She would deserve no better than to be put stark naked into a barrel into which sharp pointed nails have been hammered, which is harnessed up to two white horses and dragged up and down until she dies.' 'You are she,' said the old king, 'and you have just sentenced yourself.' And so the maid-servant was condemned to death, and the sentence carried out. But the young king married the true bride and they reigned over the kingdom together in peace and happiness.[84]

A mother promises the hand of her daughter in marriage to a king's son who lives far away. In other words, the mother makes sure that a separation between her and her daughter will happen. The girl herself – and this is unusual in fairy tales – must make a long journey to seek out the king's son. She has to learn a thing or two before she can form a relationship with him.

The treasures which the princess takes with her suggest the rich abundance of the mother complex. The white handkerchief with three drops of her mother's blood on it is a sign of the deep connection between mother and daughter, which the girl hides away close to her heart – where all valuable and secret things are kept. So here we have a young woman who is clearly formed by an originally positive mother complex. She is richly endowed with all that she could need. She has been given a vital and healthy foundation for life – expressed in the image of the horse, Falada. Horses are symbolic of the way we feel about our body, the way we make use of and deal with our different bodily energies; also of how we relate to our feelings and our unconscious. The king's daughter is strong, vital, dynamic. She is at home in her body, whose sensations and intuitions she can listen to and follow. She is also close to her unconscious, for the horse is wise and can speak to her. It seems to express the benevolent wisdom inherent in a 'mother-realm' which the girl has internalized and which she can always refer back to in need. The blood-drops on the handkerchief signify that she still has a profound, magical connection with her actual mother.

She has all that she needs; but no sooner has she set out than she falls under the sway of her own shadow, the maidservant. Like every other daughter who emerges with an originally positive mother complex, she can hardly believe that another woman could treat her so badly. It seems that the king's daughter has until now been wholly blind to her own shadow-sides, especially to her desire for power and the aggressive urges belonging to it. The feeling of totality and oneness that an originally positive mother complex strives to attain is always connected with a definite longing for power – for what is more powerful than totality? But as long as we possess this feeling of wholeness, which seems like a kind of birthright, we usually fail to see how tightly we hold on to the reins of power – especially when it is in danger of slipping out of our grasp. People with this form of complex will not need to exercise their power until their feeling of wholeness is threatened – but watch out when it is!

The king's daughter becomes completely dominated by the power-lust of her shadow. She no longer dwells in the realm of the conscious ego complex, which is still bound up with the mother complex, but has become enthralled by what was formerly banished to a safe distance and kept in a subservient role. This is why the handkerchief with its blood-drops is swept away on an inevitable flood-tide, bearing with it her close connection with her mother.

We generally emancipate ourselves from mother and father

complexes by integrating those shadow aspects rejected at the time the original complexes – and all the collective values they expressed – were formed.[85] The originally positive mother complex does not, by its very nature, accept aggression and separation, but splits them off from its ideal and banishes them. These banished aspects are contained as potential in the rejected shadow. The process of separation and emancipation causes them to rear their heads and overwhelm us. While this process is taking place, people often identify very strongly with their shadow. There are clear images of this in the story: the girl's transition from instinctual certainty to loss of instinct and direction is symbolized by the loss of her horse. The radical change in her personality, which extends to her outer appearance, is expressed in the shabby clothes she must accept from the maidservant–shadow in exchange for her rich ones. She must also swear to tell no-one about this personality change. This oath, though, gives us the first glimpse of her redemption. By swearing, she names and tells what has happened; she becomes conscious that she is not actually the maidservant, even though that is how she appears. The oath tells her that she has another identity apart from the shadow identity she has to live with for the time being.

So she has, for the present, a looser connection with the values of the mother-realm. But Falada is still in the picture – what the positive mother influence provides us with is not ultimately lost, although it may recede into the background and appear to be lost.

The young king unsuspectingly receives the false bride. A woman cannot show her true self in her first encounter with the opposite sex, nor can a young man perceive her properly. But the old, fatherly king is clearer-sighted; he sees beyond the shadow to her delicacy and beauty, which still survive beneath appearances. The relationship between the king's son and the false bride seems, outwardly, to be fine; but the relationship excludes all the richness and abundance with which the true bride is endowed.

The true bride becomes a goose-girl; she has to do a particularly mundane job. People with an originally positive mother complex do need to experience 'ordinary life', for no-one can be special and out-of-the-ordinary all the time and in all situations. The animals which are looked after in stories – and with which, therefore, the protagonists become more acquainted – tell us something about what they lack. Geese are creatures of Aphrodite; they represent erotic and sexual love and fertility. They may also, since they forage around in mud, be connected with the shadow-sides of sexuality. So an erotic and sexual realm that is seen as foreign to the mother, that belongs, rather, to the realm of the maidservant, is here 'cared for', or integrated.

The king's daughter suffers from her situation. Every morning she passes through a dark doorway on her way to open fields. The gateway suggests sadness but also hope that this situation is one to be 'passed through', one that will have an end. The false bride has Falada killed – under a pretext which the young king fails to see through. But at that point the true bride remembers her horse and begins to take the initiative. She thinks back to aspects of herself which were once unquestionably available to her; by so doing she has already begun to ascend from the depths of her shadow identity, even though nothing has yet outwardly changed. Falada's response to the pity she feels for him contains a reminder of the mother-realm; the goose-girl's empathy for her own situation helps her to reconnect with her unshadowed self. But she is no longer the same as she was. She does not flee back to the safety of the mother complex atmosphere; she has learnt to do ordinary things, to be subservient when needed. She has also connected with her sexuality. Her relationship with little Conrad on the one hand, and the old king on the other, expresses a need commonly felt by young women closely attached to their mothers, who have no father or brothers. When such a woman has a relationship with a man of her own age, it will be a shadow relationship; this is expressed in the union between the king's son and the maidservant. To start relating to a man in a real way, she will need to find access to two aspects of masculinity – perhaps in one and the same man: the playful, boyish aspect; and the fatherly. With little Conrad, the king's daughter has a teasing, erotic, flirtatious relationship. First she entices him by combing her long, shining hair, then chases him away. He complains about her behaviour to the old king.

Here we have two animus figures in the psyche of the king's daughter: the boy and the king, neither of which existed in the original complex-configuration. The old king clearly represents a connection with the father complex, whereas little Conrad embodies a newly-dawning fascination with a teasing and enticing erotic situation. The old king stands for all that is reliable, considered and traditional. He will order and regulate everything that is fluctuating and erratic. He also helps the goose-girl to express her sorrow – at least to the stove. She has to consciously formulate what has happened; but she can do it only in a totally secure and protected situation. The risk remains, perhaps, that she could still get baked in the oven, which represents the mother's womb. But through the hole in it, her words can reach beyond it to the king's ear. By expressing her pain in words, she reconnects with her mother, whose 'heart would break in two'. She formulates words, expresses her suffering and laments. By so doing she breaks the spell of her shadow identification and can become the true bride of the king's son. Unfortunately, we do not hear about *his* emancipation from the positive father complex!

This story shows us a process of emancipation from the originally positive mother complex. In this instance, the mother initiates the separation and encourages the daughter to emerge into the world, providing her with what she needs for the journey. This positive 'push' is characteristic of a good mother. The daughter is then overpowered by her shadow; this is often connected with a feeling that the mother-realm inhibits an experience of 'real life', and that an old world that was comforting and secure now no longer exists. The complex-expectation that the world should treat one like a caring mother is disappointed. In the story, the daughter reacts to this state of affairs with, on the one hand, gestures of power and aggression –

which are not, though, grounded in any real achievement or experience of life – and on the other hand with depression. The original complex-configuration recedes into unconsciousness. But in her depressive reaction, she does what needs to be done: she becomes more ordinary and develops a connection with her sexuality, at the same time finding access to an animus that is closely related to the father complex. She cannot develop further by going down the road of compensation through empty gestures of power and aggression. Instead, although her shadow has temporarily overpowered her, she recalls the old feelings of abundance and security. These enable her to strike up a relationship with a man, or at least with animus aspects which help her enter more into real life and realize her potential. Women with an originally positive mother complex have a tendency either to idealize men, or, if the shadow-sides dominate, to devalue them. In either case, they need to develop a connection with the animus. Such a woman is often sought out by a man, rather than she herself going out of her way to find one.

CHAPTER 7

The originally positive father complex of the son

'Proud father – wonderful son'

The mother complex can be so marked that the father complex fades out of the picture. In the same way, though, a father complex can dominate, leaving little room for the mother complex.

'It's good to be a man' – Frank

Frank is 49. His originally positive father complex dominates; he doesn't show much sign of a mother complex. He is not in therapy and would never consider he needed it. I'm assuming an originally positive father complex because he frequently tells me stories about himself as a young boy with his father, and he still glows with pride as he tells them. At work, he seems to be surrounded by a crowd of father-figures. He doesn't rebel against this – he's perfectly happy with it. I know him because he sometimes phones me up and asks me for a brainstorming session about something connected with his work. These session last 45 minutes – never more nor less. He did me the favour of allowing me to interview him about his father complex, partly because 'there's sure to be something worth learning from a father complex', and partly because he owed me a favour. It is characteristic of him that he knows to whom he owes a favour. I was allowed to interview him for 45 minutes.

Frank is completely at home in the world of action and outer things. He shows a lot of initiative, is hard-working, busy and dynamic. He also knows a great deal. He thinks it's a good idea to be as knowledgeable as possible and to be able to show he knows what's what at the right moment. He is happy to leave more subtle musings to philosophers and psychologists. He's not very interested in problems which can't be solved by a straightforward answer, or which can't be solved at all. He is talented: he knows this and is proud of it. He also has a definite gift of the gab; he enjoys talking – loud and long. He can hold a certain kind of woman spellbound with his conversation. Even though what he actually says is not always so significant, the way he says it carries conviction. He believes in progress, but has no time for 'crazy experiments'. This usually means that he prefers to carry on in tried and trusted ways, perhaps just with a slightly different emphasis or an increased input of activity. He knows what's right and what's wrong and finds it out by thinking himself into situations and comparing them with previous ones. He gets to grips with things, he gets other people working as well; he can be inspiring, particularly when it comes to getting something done. He is not very creative himself and knows it, but he has a great ability to realize the creative ideas of others, as long as they don't seem too risky. He is convinced that you can do anything if you set your mind to it.

He possesses a rock-solid identity: he knows that he is a real man, and he likes being one. He can see the justification for arguments about improving the role of women in society ('All people have the right to the same rights. And women, of course, are also people'), but he criticizes the 'extreme' way that pressure groups voice their opinions and demands about such things: 'After all, we've survived all right up to now.' He often talks of men who have helped him in one way or another. Even now he seems to have a circle of men who support him. Listening to him one would think that his profession contains only men, though this is not the case. He looks at reality through father complex spectacles which blank out the 30 per cent of workers in his field who are women. He likes talking about his work – he makes it seem very exciting – but one wonders to what extent his descriptions, in particular of the board of directors of his firm (of which he is a member), are idealized. However, he doesn't emphasize his own achievements at the expense of others. He paints a picture of himself as a talented, efficient man among a crowd of such exceptional men. He likes talking about his rapid and assured ascent of the career ladder; he is a bit concerned, though, that there is not much further he can go, in the next few years at any rate. When he writes reports, he substantiates his statements with copious footnotes, which take up approximately two-thirds of the text. That may make for laborious reading, but he thinks it would be a shame – and also incomplete – to omit a cross-reference.

He occasionally criticizes the patriarchal nature of society, but not to the extent of questioning his own attitudes. He merely shows that he is aware of the arguments. He doesn't really come into contact with feminists. He rarely mentions his wife and his two daughters, who come across in his conversation only as shadowy figures. He has a bit of a bad conscience, as 'a man does' when he is busy with his work and has too little time for his family.

'Father and I, we're one'

Formation of this complex

Frank's father was also an academic. He remembers that his father always seemed annoyed to be disturbed in his reading when Frank rushed into his study – until he saw that it was his son who had disturbed him. Then he broke into smiles. From an early age, Frank's father talked to him as an equal, sharing with him what he had just been reading, though it went over Frank's head. Frank didn't mind – he felt his father took him seriously. Before long they started discussing ethical problems together. His father taught him Socratic dialogue. After such discussions they would tell the women in the house that they had been busy with 'men's talk'. Sometimes Frank was allowed to accompany his father on outings and excursions with male colleagues. He particularly remembered his father making camp-fires. 'I knew I was the son of a man whom other men respected. At home I thought: "Father is the most important person in the house, and I am his only son." '

I asked Frank about his mother and two sisters: 'Mother looked after the house. She and my sisters belonged to one world, my father and I to another. When I was ill I took refuge in the mother-world, but otherwise it was unimportant. My father was the one who counted, who set the tone. My mother made sure he wasn't disturbed. Only I was allowed to disturb him – but not always of course.' Then, more reflectively, he said: 'When I held my father's hand and walked along beside him, I used to think: "Father and I, we're one, we're part of each other." ' This phrase is reminiscent of one of Jesus's sayings.[86]

I asked him to describe any other accompanying feelings he had had. 'I felt like I *was* someone; I wanted to show the world I could become someone like my father. Perhaps I thought that I would like to prove myself worthy of him.'

I asked him whether he had felt whole and secure, protected from the world. But he said that it was rather a feeling of pride, of having 'backbone'; a feeling of being important.

So in this case we have an originally positive father complex, formed through a father who represents the collective norm – a significant authority figure who stimulated in his son an awareness of cultural and social traditions, who gave him clear guidance and inspired him.

I asked Frank about conflicts. He said that for a short while during his adolescence he had expressed different political opinions to his father. He had had to adopt a very extreme position because his father was far from being a blinkered conservative; he had a strong sense of justice and of the rights of the under-dog. On one occasion Frank had clearly expressed opposite opinions to his father, but can no longer remember the subject of debate. He remembers, though, that his father had argued him into a corner, and then ended the discussion with the phrase: 'You have the duty to think independently! But if you turn your back on certain values in the process, I can't be proud of you any longer.'

The originally positive mother complex forbids leaving. The originally positive father complex, on the other hand, withdraws its feeling of pride about an offspring who rejects its values and ideas.

Some of the difficulties inherent in this sort of situation have become apparent in Frank's current relationship with his now 80-year-old father: 'My father is still proud of me, but on various occasions he's said he's had about enough of telling me what a wonderful son I am.' Frank also no longer adores his father, who has grown old and forgetful, almost a bit pitiful. His father still writes, but with none of the old fire and sharpness. He sends these texts to his relations, but they are 'mystical' and embarrass Frank. 'I can't see anything in him to look up to now, but luckily there are other men of whom I stand in awe.'

Frank's relationship with his father was based on mutual admiration and adoration. Although this has now ebbed, Frank still projects it upon other male figures. This leaves him still in the role of a son, dependent on a father's appreciation. He behaves in such a way that the 'fathers' who surround him can be proud of him and do not feel threatened by him. By supporting these fathers he simultaneously supports his own self-esteem. He's not interested in helping and encouraging a younger generation; he's far more focused upon the old guard. This poses a problem, for: 'What do you do when you've reached the top and there's nowhere else to go except down?'

A further problem is his unquestioning acceptance of the authority of the 'fathers'. He accommodates himself to their views – and this annoys many of his peers, who consider that he is being sycophantic and also failing to see that there are things which need to change. Frank thinks these colleagues are jealous and immature. He also stands aloof from rivalry with the up-and-coming generation, for he is sure that his position is unassailable. He has invested much energy in his fixation on the role of son and does not yet realize this. His attitude to old age is also problematic: he cannot find anything positive in the changes he sees in his father.

I also think that his relationship to women is unbalanced. It seems astonishing that he is not aware of this. Men with an originally positive father complex tend to find it problematic when women rebel and do not keep to their 'allotted' place.

Frank does not seem at ease in his present circumstances: he describes them as 'very strenuous'. He still basks in a fair amount of recognition, but to maintain it he has to exert himself more and more. Men and women with a dominating father complex typically feel that they must achieve a great deal to earn love and respect. And, despite this effort and respect, they are still denied an oceanic experience of wholeness. They cannot achieve harmony in their lives by determination and effort. They are much more likely to find it if they manage to relax and turn inwards to a world of imagination – though this is unlikely to happen unless such a world can be seen to have a 'use'. It would be important for Frank to explore his feminine aspects, to free them from the insignificance in which they are imprisoned and somehow integrate them into his life. Also to become conscious of his own shadow-sides, rather than just project them onto others. It may be that his existence as a son will exhaust him too much. He might have some kind of breakdown, which could be an opportunity for him to become aware of the dominating father complex that confines him. Men like Frank find it very hard to accept that they have missed out on a necessary developmental stage. They are successful, respected, expert in their chosen field – and what they are not expert in is seen to be of little worth, even by the rest of society. In such a complex, as in all complex-configurations, a man can identify more with the father than with the son aspect. It is then often very hard to tell whether emancipation has taken place or not – whether the son is simply very similar in various ways to his father, or is stuck in a complex-identification.

'Rock-solid people' – Bruno

Bruno, 45 years old, is a tradesman. He has just taken over his father's business. He seems very solid and reliable, proud of his profession and work. He keeps saying how much he owes his father. He is proud when his customers say that he takes after him, that he, too, is trustworthy and efficient. Bruno tells me all this, though the consultation is actually about his daughter, who is 'right out of line'. She doesn't want to finish her schooling, doesn't want to 'do' anything at all in fact; she reproaches her parents with being horribly old-fashioned and says she wouldn't mind running away from home. All the 'fuss and bother' she is causing is 'spoiling the other three children'. 'Heaven knows what's got into her,' says Bruno, 'we're rock-solid people, we're decent folk, we work hard for our living.' 'Exactly,' sums up their 17-year-old daughter. She is clearly pleased to have made her parents desperate enough to arrange this consultation. It's also obvious that she will succeed in breaking the grip which a dominating father complex has on this family. No wonder, then, that the father feels compelled to list all that is good about it. During the sessions, his daughter shows him that he has never fulfilled a 'single desire of his own', that he hasn't even allowed himself to have any, but has only fulfilled his father's wishes. Bruno is certainly very reliable and consistent, conservative in the best sense, without being pig-headed. But his daughter has hit the nail on the head when she accuses him of having missed out on his own life, of being just an imitation of her grandfather – whom, incidentally, she seems to respect and love. The mother sits there quietly during the consultation, saying nothing unless I address her directly, and then only backing up her husband's views. She also fails to understand why, in a family in which the womenfolk have always been 'meek and mild', one of them should suddenly get so 'uppish'. She doesn't have much understanding for the idea that it might be high time for such a woman to express herself more radically. She blames the school her daughter attends, and the times in general.

'You can do what you set your mind to'

Similarities and differences between two sons with an originally positive father complex

We have here two different forms of positive father complex: one is more fatherly, the other more motherly. In neither case is there is any apparently urgent need for emancipation, for both have a secure identity, albeit of a rather inflexible kind. Their ego complex seems coherent and assured, closely identified with the father complex – which in our society still tends to define collective values of what is normal and desirable. But neither of them have a real identity of their own; they cannot become themselves because their complex dictates the father-values they must abide by if they are to remain successful and worthy of recognition.

Both of these men seem fully integrated and at home in a man's world. They are successful, pragmatic, hard working, efficient. They have a basic belief that they can 'do what they set their mind to'. This also implies, though, an unconscious ideology of control, of minimizing risk through a firm code of values. They are capable of persuading themselves and others that the world is 'under control', that they have their guiding hands on life's steering wheel.

They are very unaware of their own fears. These only surface when there is some threat to their feeling of being in control: at times of illness, for instance, or when relationship problems arise which cannot be sorted out in a 'reasonable way', or when they are faced with the thought of growing old. When such difficulties appear, they are confronted by a devalued feminine world; a man whose father was influenced by a mother complex will find this far easier, for he is already half way there. Breakdowns and depressions can occur and give an impetus for a man to seek a real foundation for his life, a real connection with his suppressed feelings. Anxiety and fear in such men have been kept at bay by the mechanisms of control and obsession – which also suppress creativity.

Such men are compelled by a constant, unconscious desire to achieve in order to win recognition and acceptance. Although they feel that they have a 'very good life', they are unconsciously aware of their unsatisfied, fundamental need for wholeness and harmony.

CHAPTER 8

Dutiful daughters

*The originally positive
father complex in women*

A daughter's father complex is naturally affected by the mother or father complex of her father. It seems to me that the father–daughter connection is maintained for longer if the father has a positive mother complex, because this has erotic undertones. There follow two examples of the different ways in which an originally positive father complex comes to expression. These also show that the father complex can reveal itself both in relationship to actual men and to the 'male' aspects of culture, expressed in norms, values and intellectual pursuits.

'Men are just more interesting' – Nora

Nora is 34. I have called her Nora for a good reason – in reference to Ibsen's play *Nora* or *The Doll's House*. She got married at 19, has 3 children and goes out to work for 10 hours a week. She looks very young and it is hard to believe that she is the mother of three quite old children. She is dressed very fashionably; but she wears high-heel shoes, which are not necessarily in vogue these days. We smile at each other as she comes clicking on them up my garden path: 'The things one does for the sake of men,' she says. But there isn't a single man anywhere on the horizon.

Nora is looking for help in a relationship crisis. She has fallen in love with an older man, a teacher who 'holds the most wonderful lectures'. She is worried what this might mean for her marriage. Neither the teacher nor her husband are aware of the situation, but Nora feels 'shaken up'. Her conversation is full of phrases like: 'My husband says . . . my husband has decided . . . my husband wants . . . ,' but also: 'As my father would say . . . my father thinks . . . .' She says that she specially chose a woman therapist because in the presence of men she becomes 'stupid', loses her will-power and sense of self, and starts to flirt – usually with success. She is able to reflect quite coolly on her behaviour with men but unable to alter this behaviour. She has written down a list of questions that she wants to ask me. 'I'm always fascinated by older men,' she says. 'Does that mean I have a father complex? If so, what should I do about it?'

Nora is lively, happy with the world and herself. She seems to be a practical, down-to-earth woman, interested and alert, and very structured in her conversation. To such an extent, in fact, that our conversation seems more like a question and answer game than an open dialogue in which there might be room for something creative and unexpected to occur. She has a tendency to file away my answers as though they come from a high authority – sometimes she actually writes them down word for word. She frequently reports back to me on her father's or one of her teachers' reactions to things I have said. Since their reactions show me, apparently, to be generally 'reasonable' ('for a woman', I feel like adding!), she starts relaxing and trusting me a bit more. It is hard to get hold of what she herself thinks about anything. Her falling in love, though, is symptomatic of something more individual breaking through. It doesn't fit in with the rest of her stuctured pattern.

Nora is friendly, but a little cool and distant. This is, she says, because I am a woman. She would behave differently with a man. It is easier to find out what a man wants to hear. Things are more clear-cut with men: they are in a position of authority, and she is there to learn from them. In our sessions she treats me a little like a man, because of my training and professional role. She is very irritated when I ask whether there is nothing to be learnt from women. Theoretically there is, of course. But in practice she has always learnt everything from men. You can also flirt a little with men, that makes everything easier and more pleasant, 'oils the wheels' of conversation.

'The things one does for the sake of men'
The formation and effect of this father complex

Nora says: 'I am my father's only daughter.' This phrase, and the way she says it, is in itself something of a give-away, though she herself notices nothing unusual about it. She and her father had always very much loved and admired one another. He showed openly, in public, how proud he was of her; and she tried to earn this pride in every possible way. Between her and her mother there was a certain competitiveness. Nora was only happy when she was sure of first place in her father's affections. She was continually testing her position: 'I think I probably always behaved like that, but I can distinctly remember it at about the age of ten. Whenever I had the feeling that my mother and father were getting close in a way that excluded me, I would begin to cry or whine. Then my father would rush into my room to comfort me; sometimes he even lay down and slept beside me. That filled me with pride.' Here we have a close, idealized father–daughter relationship of mutual admiration while the mother–daughter relationship is pushed into the background. Although her memories are of a relatively late stage of childhood, she also has family snapshots of herself as an infant, in which she and her father look lovingly and joyfully at one another while the mother remains at a certain distance.

When she was 16, she often went dancing with her father. Her mother didn't enjoy dancing. She remembers that she worked much harder for teachers who took an interest in her than for those who didn't. 'Men always had the power to further or hinder my studies.' Nowadays she finds this astonishing and alarming. She also remembers that her father was always jealous of the teachers she liked. If we were to formulate a complex-phrase for Nora, it would be: 'Never admire anyone more than me.'

Men are very important to her. They stimulate, guide, control; they also permit her to be a little childish and to show and make use of her charm, which helps her get on in life. The fact that she married quite young may be connected with a tendency, dictated by the originally positive father complex, to behave conventionally. She also wears fashionable clothing, not primarily because she likes it, but because it is the 'done' thing.

Her husband was a student who had been working in her father's business. Her father had said on several occasions that he would have liked a son like him – as well as his beloved daughter of course. At her wedding she danced more with her father than with her 'new husband'. Her father was very pleased with her choice, as she was herself. When such an erotically charged atmosphere exists between father and daughter, they are both likely to feel relieved when the danger of erotic temptation between them recedes.

Nora proved to be very compliant and obliging in her marriage. She had learnt to be so from her father. First of all she helped her husband sort out the 'chaos' in his life; she got him to finish writing his thesis. She tells me how she responded to his needs: 'My husband needed me to be many different kinds of woman at different times. At first he desired a companion and friend. Then, when things weren't going so well for him, he needed a mother. When they improved he wanted me to be more flirtatious and sexual. I became whatever he needed.' You can hear in her voice her pride at being so versatile. She was pleased when her husband told her that she was 'like wax in his hands'. When I ask her which role she felt most at ease in, or most discomfort with, she is unable to reply. It all suited her fine. It was fun. She is proud that she and her husband have a good relationship. At work things are rather different. There she is surrounded by other women and she behaves in a more independent and decisive way; she is more critical and on the

ball than at home, where she simply responds to her husband's
wishes. This is typical of the originally positive father complex:
such women can be innovative, independent and politically
active outside the realm of influence of their complex. They
know men very well and therefore also know how to manoeuvre
themselves into powerful positions. But in a personal relationship with a man, they revert to being obliging (or in some cases
rebellious) girls.

Once a week Nora has dinner alone with her father. Her
mother 'is not and never has been important'. She does not
remember having any particular conflict with her. It was just
'clear from the beginning that my Dad was the important one'.
Recently her mother has been criticizing her a bit, saying she's
such an 'old-fashioned sort of woman'. Some of her less close
women friends have been saying the same. A clear sign, though,
that it is time for her to free herself from her originally positive
father complex is that she is increasingly fearful of making
decisions about her personal life. Several times she has fallen in
love with older men and experienced feelings she never felt with
her husband. These unforeseen episodes show that her psyche
is calling for a change in her father complex pattern. Whereas
her father is a man of action like her husband, the men she is
falling in love with are 'men of words'. Her fascination is not so
much with these older men themselves, but with an aspect of
the father complex – an intellectual aspect – that she has until
now had little experience of. She is faced with a difficulty: her
complex-constellation dictates that she shall regard no-one
more highly than her father. She has probably extended this to
include her husband; it is her relationship with him that she is,
no doubt rightly, worried about. As she frees herself from the
father complex and its projection upon her husband, she will
find out what affection, if any, is left to carry the relationship
forward. She *must* free herself, though, for her fear and anxiety
show that she is in danger of missing out an important developmental stage in her life.

It is highly probable that Nora's father has an originally
positive mother complex. I do not know to what extent he freed

himself from this at the proper time. Fathers who have a positive mother complex are sensual and erotic; they enjoy life and
also, of course, enjoy their daughters. They need to be looked
up to and admired; and it is often easier for them to be assured
of their daughters' admiration than that of their wives.

Daughters who identify with the daughter aspect of this
complex-constellation, who make themselves into the attractive
daughters of a god-like father, become women who have a
power of erotic attraction over men and make use of it. They
are often intellectually gifted but undervalue their ability; or
they have learnt to conceal it and only to use it when necessary.
They have been much admired by their fathers and therefore
have a positive self-image. But they have experienced neither
solidarity nor confrontation with their mothers, who have
simply been devalued. They would never admit this though,
preferring to say that they just find men more interesting,
stimulating, reliable . . . They are unlikely even to notice that
they have never in their lives really opened themselves up to the
feminine.

Such women need the admiration of men to preserve their
self-esteem. But this is very problematic, for they are then
dependent on those who value them. Losing them means losing
this self-esteem. The more we let ourselves be controlled and
guided by others, the greater is the danger of being steered off
course, away from the path our own developmental needs
require.

There is an added danger that people who have always looked
to others for guidance are filled with fear when such guidance
ceases,[87] for they have never learnt to make decisions for themselves. At the mid-life point at the latest, such women suddenly
feel 'empty'. They do not know what they themselves need or
want, but feel themselves to be at the mercy of outside forces,
whose influence they are unable to counteract with positive
forces of their own. Even small decisions about relatively
insignificant things may fill them with anxiety. In other words,
they have not learnt to take responsibility for themselves, nor to
face and cope with the consequences of wrong decisions.

Their fear is also ultimately tied up with the fact that they cannot be themselves, that their true self is in some sense excluded from life. This fear is often repressed or expressed in physical symptoms, for a 'father's daughter' is not meant to be afraid. If the fear does surface, they often become even more dependent on someone else to help and guide them, and this in turn hinders them from coming to terms with their complex-pattern. But it is very hard for such a woman to admit her fear to herself. As she identifies so closely with the father aspect of her father complex, she will often appear to have a strong, well-structured ego complex, to be reasonable and able to cope. This will be true as far as 'outer' life is concerned, but her inner state and her developmental needs will be in turmoil. Her identity and her ego strength are borrowed from her father; they are not fully her own.[88] But one of our most essential developmental tasks is to discover and continually strengthen our own identity during the course of our life.

One can also see a collective influence at work in this complex-configuration. Until a few years ago, Nora would have been seen as a woman who embodied the ideal role of a woman. That is not necessarily so any longer; even her mother now reproaches her with being an 'old-fashioned kind of woman'. It is alarming, though, that an image of woman which allowed no room for self-discovery should have been held up as an ideal. Such an image did no-one any good: neither women nor men, neither children nor marriages – even if it might appear on the surface to have been a convenient and advantageous state of affairs.

'Lacking in warmth' – Anne

Fathers who have been moulded by a father complex do not, on the whole, have daughters who rely on them in a close personal way. Their daughters identify more with the father complex atmosphere, although the actual father and his significant inter-actions with her can still provide a personal context.

Anne is 34 years old. She is an academic and holds a leading position in a therapeutic institution. Although her colleagues find her reliable, fair and competent, they also experience her as not 'human' enough, too controlling and anxious. They complain that she is not a very warm person and that she insists too much on her own authority.

Anne is pondering this feedback. She knows that such complaints are not simply objective descriptions of her. Since they arise from an interactional process they are coloured by her colleagues' expectations and ideas about what she should be like. But the accusation that she is not warm and human enough has struck home. She wants to explore this problem in psychoanalytical sessions, because she experiences herself as too controlled and controlling in her private life. She is also, though, subject to periodic outbreaks of emotion. She lives alone and has a network of friends – but they are not particularly close to her. She also still keeps up contact with her family and likes spending time with her numerous sisters. In our sessions together she seems rather aloof and distant; she formulates her problem in a clear and careful way. She is ruthlessly honest in analysing herself, and when she finds something that she does not like, she wants to eradicate it immediately. She is very trustworthy, responsible and intelligent, but she has to analyse everything with great precision, which is actually a symptom of her anxiety. She is very well educated and proud of her knowledge and ability, but she says that she is no good at solving problems on the spot. She seems to be a woman with a very strong and coherent ego complex.

It is noticeable that she has to satisfy her own very rigid norms and values. If she is unable to do so she is plagued with self-doubt and anxiety – which she keeps at bay by trying to control a situation even more. It is characteristic of these rigid values that she looks up to others for authority (although this is not immediately obvious), and that she herself makes an authoritative impression. She is more aware of being dependent on authority than of being one herself. She feels ashamed that she sometimes throws out her own ideas, at least temporarily, and hangs on someone else's every word instead. Her work is valued more highly by others than by herself. She is dedicated and innovative, but she evidently has high expectations of herself which she finds it difficult to fulfil. Her colleagues certainly recognize her positive qualities, as well as the lack of human warmth.

Anne is quite hard on herself. When talking about changing herself she shows the kind of hard-grafting determination which deals in phrases like: 'It must be possible; if not, it's due to a lack of willingness or effort.' And: 'Where there's a will there's a way!'

She is sure that you can only win someone's affection by giving them what they need; she is surprised that she has not yet found a lover, for she believes that she has a lot to give. She meets plenty of men, but they all lose interest in her after a short while. When she asks them why they withdraw emotionally from her, the usual reply is: 'There's just no spark between us.' She is honest enough to admit that she is not a very exciting person; sometimes she wishes she had more time to devote to herself – then, she thinks, she might eventually develop a spark or two. So far love has not really come her way – only steady friendships. Anne is an ideal chum for a man who wants a shoulder to cry on or get some good advice. She is a good, uncomplicated companion – but nothing more.

'Anyone who can't grasp that is useless'

Formation and effect of this father complex

Anne is the eldest of four children. Her father very much wanted a son, but had to wait for his youngest child to fulfil this wish. Nevertheless he was very happy with his clever daughter, although he did not spend all that much time with her. He was a lawyer and the conversation at mealtimes often revolved around matters of law. Anne remembers that truth, justice and order were very important themes, as well as ideas about 'moderation'. Anne always felt very important when she was allowed to go for a walk alone with her father and reply to his questions about how things were going at school. She remembers that she learnt to judge whether something was right or wrong in the light of his questions. She adopted his masculine way of thinking, which implied that there are rules which must be observed. Her father rejected the idea that rules might need to be adapted to particular situations. She remembers that one of her class-mates had told a lie to protect her best friend, who was less able and whom she thought the teacher picked on – and was caught out. Anne felt that this lie was different from one that you told for your own sake, but her father insisted that all lying was bad. Anne accepted and adopted his point of view. Modern psychological research shows that her argument in this instance is representative of a typically feminine form of thinking, which takes account of the whole context and the relative factors of a situation.[89]

Anne derived her self-esteem to a large extent from the rather sparing esteem her father showed her. Her mother was much more affirming and gentle towards her, but she did not value this so much – she wanted her father's love. Anne remembers her father as a man who demanded much of himself and severely criticized himself when he did not do things as well as he wanted. He has since become gentler, both with himself and his family. But Anne internalized a father complex whose stern demands she is constrained to fulfil, and which makes her life somewhat joyless. Although she appears, outwardly, to have separated herself quite distinctly from her father, her originally positive father complex still denies her access to particular areas of life – to warm emotions and to a feeling of being close to others without having to do anything to deserve it.

One image from her childhood clearly illuminates the personal aspect of her father complex. She sees herself sitting with her father at a stone table. She knows that it is stone because her father had told her it would last much longer than wood; but she herself doesn't like touching it. She remembers her father saying in a suddenly rather heated way – which was unusual for him: 'Anyone who can't grasp that is useless.' The child Anne then felt herself to be very small, knowing that if she insisted she preferred sitting at a wooden table, her father would consider her 'useless'. She knew what that meant; she had often heard her father calling various people 'useless'. Her father, she also knew, was not speaking personally to her or asking her to agree with him about the better quality of stone. In other words he had deserted the personal realm and was speaking on a collective level. Therefore Anne felt excluded from her desired relationship with her father, even if she decided to sacrifice her own preference for wood.

Her father's 'reasonable opinions' had therefore to be shared at any price, otherwise she risked a double banishment: she would be designated 'useless' and she would no longer be addressed by him in a personal way. This experience made her feel very lonely and made drastic inroads into her self-esteem. She had no alternative but to adopt the opinions of her father. But she was never sure, as a child, whether she had done this sufficiently, for her father never gave her any signs of affirmation. Anne therefore always retained a feeling of not having quite done enough, of not being able to be wholly happy with herself.

She herself supposes that she is closely identified with the father aspect of her father complex, which explains why her colleagues often feel that they cannot live up to her demands. But she still experiences herself much more in the child's position. She is gradually learning to praise her colleagues when they have done something well. She sees the need for this, but also realizes her marked tendency to imitate her father's lack of warm response. As we explored the messages of her unconscious, it became obvious that she was trying to control everything she received in this way, to order and name it. When images and figures arose – animus elements such as the fascinating, mysterious stranger, which she desperately needed to help her bring neglected areas of her psyche to consciousness – it was very difficult indeed for her to simply let them affect her, to accept the fantasies which appeared and to allow the emotions associated with them to reverberate in her. Her tendency was to file them into 'compartments'. Only gradually did she come to realize that by doing so she was confining and circumscribing the abundance which her dreams were providing, that she was transforming it into rigid definitions that left her once more unnourished, that gave her a sense, again, of not having 'done well enough'. This sense was in some ways accurate, for although she was proceeding with great care and determination, she was applying the wrong method. She gradually learnt instead to enter more into the images from her unconscious. They began to open up a 'new world' for her, in which she could dwell, in which achievement and categorization were no longer so important. Simultaneously she began to show more interest in her mother. She started talking to her and also remembering episodes from her childhood in which her mother had played a part – episodes which had previously been obscured.

Hard-working schoolgirls

Common attributes of women with an originally positive father complex

Women with an originally positive father complex find older men attractive. Those whose father was moulded by a positive mother complex tend to seek out older men with erotic charms, while those with a father influenced by a positive father complex are more interested in a platonic relationship. Neither type of woman say much about themselves. Their attention is not focused upon themselves, even if this is not immediately obvious. One type may say: 'My husband says . . . ,' while the other is more likely to speak eloquently about the achievements of particular men. Both kinds are usually hard-working school-girls and students. If they are not particularly creative, they can easily become very schoolmistressy. Their mother complex is often devalued and pushed into the background. If so, they are convinced that no-one can achieve anything in this world without enormous effort, that nothing will be given them if they do not work for it – love least of all. At the same time as idealizing all things male, they devalue themselves as women without noticing it. Not only men but also theories, knowledge and beliefs easily become absolute standards, sometimes even a sort of holy doctrine.

Such women are actually far more dependent than they would otherwise be. They may be capable and confident in their chosen field and in life in general; but the moment they are in the company of men, they become dutiful daughters. Many men of course like this state of affairs, which becomes yet another reason for women to perpetuate it. In such a situation, women make out that they are more slow-witted than they really are. The daughter of a father influenced by a father, though, finds it harder to make this sort of position correspond with her self-image. She therefore tries to avoid situations in which she must assume a daughter role.

A woman who has not been able to separate herself sufficiently from a positive father complex will allow herself to be defined by male values, and her identity to be dictated to her either by a man or by some authority or intellectual approach. She no doubt invests the male principle with such authority because her self-esteem depends on her father's opinion of her. But the father cannot ultimately provide the necessary affirmation. A woman's identity must be sought through herself as a woman, through involvement with other women – whom this type of woman defends herself from and competes with – and through coming to terms with the mother and motherly qualities.

Benevolent law and order

The father-gods: a digression

It is not only individual fathers with their own father complexes who affect the configuration of a father complex. There is also a collective father-image which still sees the father as an embodiment of the 'hero in a thousand forms'.[90] 'A father's significance for an individual child often contrasts strangely with the degree of actual work he puts into the relationship with his offspring.

He often assumes a far more significant role than he deserves, because of the patriarchal nature of society and because he is idealized by women. There is, it is true, a generation of 'new men'; but they will not be able to change the traditional father-image so quickly, though they may well create some unease and disturbance in received traditions about the father's role, which could help bring about an awakening. It will be interesting to see the effect of 'new fathers' upon the complexes of their children, for a wide gulf will exist between the actual father and other, more old-fashioned father-images. (A conversation over-heard between two 5-year-olds: 'My Dad can mend things.' 'Bikes, do you mean?' 'No everything: socks, jeans, shirts . . . ' 'Then he's not a proper Dad . . . ')

There are many father-gods of cultural tradition who still, as archetypes, influence our father-image. But it seems to me important not to let such archetypal aspects make us forget social ones. It would be too easy to cite the archetypal, 'typically human' attributes of present-day fatherhood in order to falsely justify and perpetuate them. The image and the role of the father do need to change.

Nevertheless I would like to describe three father-gods who seem to me to tell us something about certain constant, archetypal qualities in our images of the father. Such images, though, should be susceptible to the transforming influence of actual life.[91]

Homer continually describes Zeus as 'benevolent and gentle as a father'. Zeus is the ruler and regulator of divine and human life. But he cannot overrule the Moirai, the goddesses of destiny who make the ultimate decisions about whether someone lives or dies. He is therefore a figure who controls conscious, active life, not an other-worldly kind of god. His style of ruling also deals out punishment and strokes of lightning when necessary. Like all father-gods he is not lacking in emotion: he frequently lets his feelings out of the bag in a raging thunderstorm directed at mortals and immortals alike. But he is also a liberated spirit and, in particular, a sexual adventurer. Homer tells us that Zeus imposes fatherly order: that is, a structured, moral, spiritual attitude to life. But his morality is chiefly one which he demands of others. He also has an originally positive mother complex – if such a thing can be said of a god. In Minoan legend, Rhea hid him from his father Kronos, who was in the habit of devouring his children. Rhea also seduced Zeus – as one might expect of a great goddess and her beloved son.[92]

Odin or Wotan, also named All-Father, is a familiar figure from Nordic mythology. He is a god of war, but does not take part in war himself, and a god of ecstatic states. The name Wotan is etymologically connected with the word for anger, which can have an ecstatic quality. He is also a god of wisdom and poetry. With his slouch-brimmed hat and his cloak sewn with stars, he wanders through the world to make sure all things are well-ordered. He checks on people's hospitality, for instance; and now and then he sits upon his throne to have a wide vista, an overview of all that is happening, while his two ravens report on what is going on. He is not immortal; in other words the order he represents and strives to impose, and his whole creativity as well, only belongs to a certain circumscribed period.

In Christianity we find a change in the image of the father-god. In the New Testament, God's relationship with human beings becomes more personal: he is the father of Jesus, who represents humanity. Jesus has, or would have if he were a human being, an originally positive father complex. His emancipation occurs on the cross, when he says: 'My God, why hast thou forsaken me?' Betrayal by our father or mother throws us back upon our own ego complex, forces us to take our individual destiny into our own hands. Something of a change occurs between the Old and New Testaments: the father-god who dispenses a fixed and undeviating set of laws becomes more benevolent.

It is apparent that all these gods are characterized by power and energy. They strive for an overview and try to impose order – which must, though, be continually re-created and defined. In other words, they express an urge to bring order into what is often seen as the chaos and arbitrariness of emotional life, so as to control it. We can discover longings for such a quality in our own father projections: we may find ourselves wishing for someone who has an overview, who understands life, or who will at least not give up the attempt to understand it; someone who will dispense a benevolent authority and show us the laws according to which our life can become more predictable. A good deal of this longing is projected onto the patriarchy of science, or onto politicians or individual men who have some leading role. That is why men who appear authoritative so easily find followers. They promise to fulfil a longing which actual fathers have mostly failed to fulfil. What people fail to realize is that – since such fatherly qualities are 'archetypal' and therefore available to the psyche of each one of us (though in perhaps slightly different ways for men than women) – everyone should be able to develop their own capacity for 'fatherliness' and integrate it into their own life. Yet alongside this capacity I believe that we also urgently need to develop motherly qualities, which infuse an awareness of relationship and relativity into what otherwise remains too abstract and prescriptive.

The father as 'other'

His role in developmental psychology

According to classical developmental psychology,[93] the father's function is to help the child find a way out of the close symbiotic relationship between mother and child. Bovensiepen, who is opposed to the patriarchal attribution to the father of authority, order, mental vigour and normative values, speaks of the father's capacity to 'initiate developmental processes and act as a catalyst for change in the father–mother–child relationship'.[94] This initiating capacity is not far removed from the energy input of the father-gods. But we must realize that two background images underpin and dominate developmental psychology: the mother, who 'holds her child back', is seen as a 'death principle'; the father, who provides impetus and energy, is thought to represent the urge for life.[95]

This categorization is rather surprising. It agrees neither with reality nor mythology, but serves to idealize the father and devalue the mother. Both, surely, can provide impetus and energy. Of course, if the mother delegates this quality to the father, because 'that's how things ought to be', then the father will have to provide it alone. It is also natural that fathers give an impetus in a slightly different way from mothers. However, recent research into infant behaviour shows that the theory of symbiosis, which underpinned the idea of the father as emancipator, has no foundation. An exclusive symbiotic phase as such does not occur, at least not to begin with; the father is also very much in the picture.[96]

Even without awareness of these results, one could imagine that having a second important figure to relate to would help to broaden the child's concepts and expectations of the world. In complex-theory this would mean that a single complex would not be able to dominate the psyche. This would make the child more flexible, would make it easier for him or her to come to terms with new situations. It would also facilitate an easier emancipation from the mother complex. But the father would not have to represent collective norms and authority to achieve this,[97] he would need only to have a relationship to the child which is different from the mother's. Later on, when the child was older, the father and mother's different ways of relating to the world would complement and be compared with each other.

The fascinating stranger

Developing the animus

As well as the ego complex, the anima – the alluring, mysterious feminine principle in a person's psyche – must be developed if emancipation from the mother complex is to take place at the right time. To begin with it is bound up with the mother complex and formed by it; but its more hidden aspects can lead one away from constriction within a complex towards new, far less circumscribed forms and images.[98] We can say that in the anima the mother complex lives out its fantasies.

The same is true of the animus, the image in our psyche of all things male which have a mysterious, fascinating quality. It is also bound up with the father complex and coloured by specific experiences. If we manage to find access to the animus aspects which express the 'fascinating stranger' and are therefore not dictated by the father complex, the corresponding images and figures which arise in our dreams and fantasies, or the projections we have of real people, will help us develop beyond it. The animus forms then cease to express an exclusive preoccupation with the father; they may become brotherly or old and wise figures, or images of the fascinating stranger as such.[99] This alluring figure, unlike some of the other, more traditionally father-like animus images, could give us some possibility of transcending patriarchal influences. This form of the animus is connected with the allure of love, or fascination with an idea. It brings with it a longing to permeate life with ideas and spirit, to strike fire from stone, to be absorbed in a great erotic or spiritual passion. To be transported in flights of the imagination and spirit belongs just as much to the animus as grasping hold of life in a concentrated and aggressive fashion. The more the animus distinguishes itself from both the collective and personal father complex, the more creative do people become. But in the animus constellation, we are still in danger of becoming too abstract and idealistic, of following rules rather than listening to feelings.

When the anima is developed simultaneously, though, a more benevolent, relative law comes into effect. The anima provides us with an emotional foundation in which we have a sense of being part of an interconnected network of life; it has a more horizontal, soulful dimension.

CHAPTER 9

The originally negative mother complex in women

'A rotten person in a rotten world'

People with an originally negative mother complex typically feel that they must make great and strenuous efforts to have any hope of their needs being met. The undemanding love, nourishment, protection, care and attention provided by an originally positive mother complex is replaced with feelings of loneliness, of being at the mercy of life, of deprivation and insufficiency.

'No right to exist' – Helma

A 44-year-old woman – whom I will call Helma – works in one of the caring professions. She is the second eldest of eight brothers and sisters. The home atmosphere when she was growing up is typical of an originally negative mother complex: 'It felt like living in a railway station. People running about all over the place, but everyone alone. It was cold and draughty at home; I always had a cold and stomach-aches, and my eyes were stuck down every morning – they had to be bathed with camomile before they'd open. Everyone wolfed down their food – there was always too little of it and it wasn't very appetizing. Our father used to leave us for weeks at a time to go and work. I would have liked to go with him – I was sure that he kept leaving because things were so dreadful at home. At 6 o'clock each evening we were shut up in a room. I can remember that I often got a wet bottom from sitting down on full potties. We used to dig holes in the wall above our beds for hours at a time. We, me and my brothers and sisters, often quarrelled with each other. Everything was a struggle somehow, we were struggling to survive.'

She still has a vivid memory of complex-phrases that she heard from infancy onwards: 'Don't touch me!/Go away!/Leave the others alone!/I'll kill you!/That's just what we'd expect of you – you're not even our child, they made a mistake at the hospital.' These are all phrases of rejection. They were commonplace throughout Helma's childhood and made her feel that she had no right to exist.

She tells me a later memory, from her schooldays: 'I was very keen on the teacher although she was actually quite mean to me. She wrote harsh things in my books, like: "You could do better if you tried. You don't concentrate enough." But at least she didn't hit me. My mother didn't like the fact that I was fond of this teacher. She used to say: "You're completely naive. People don't tell you what they really think of you."' Whenever Helma tried to make friends with other children at school, her mother would say: 'You don't need friends, you've got your brothers and sisters; and there's house-work waiting for you at home.'

From an early age, Helma was 'given away' to her mother's sister – or so it seemed to her – for indefinite periods of time. Eventually she no longer knew where she belonged. Later on she said she didn't want to go there any more, because her uncle and aunt always used to 'examine' her vagina. When her mother heard this, her only reaction was to say: 'That must be your fault. You're sure to become a tart when you're older.' When she was eight, her father sexually abused her. To begin with she very much liked creeping into bed with him and being alone together with him, being caressed. Then suddenly 'it hurt so much'; she was deeply shocked and frightened by the new turn of events. She wanted to talk to her mother about it, but the only response she got was: 'It's not nice to speak about such things. You're becoming a tart, there's no doubt about it.'

Helma's originally negative mother complex made her feel she was 'a bad person who ought not to exist. I was completely at the mercy of life, helpless and alone. I was forbidden to have any friendship with people outside the family although that is what I longed for. Whenever I struck up some kind of friendship, my mother found a way of sabotaging it.'

In contrast to the feelings of self-reliance and security provided by an originally positive mother complex, the originally negative mother complex creates distrust, anxiety and a deeply ingrained sense of having no right to exist. Helma said: 'When I was a child, life seemed so cold and such a struggle. I thought it would always be so and that I would always be bad.' That is a description of an existential mistrust of life. Instead of being sustained by a shared family context which is then transposed onto a harmonious feeling for life, there is a sense here of shared imprisonment and separation from the outer world. No 'oceanic' union with others is possible, only isolation and anxiety. The infant develops to a large extent through identification with parents. But in such a case this identification is counteracted and sabotaged. There is a permanent feeling of rejection although no final, absolute rejection occurs. This state of affairs gives rise to rivalry, for such a complex makes one feel that everything must be striven for, even survival itself. But oceanic feelings are never created by effort – they are simply 'given'.

In the atmosphere Helma describes there is no physical care and attention; instead there are illnesses – constant colds, etc – and no wonder! The atmosphere is also sexually charged, as if sexuality were the only possible level on which the body could come into its own. When Helma began to menstruate at the age of 16 – comparatively late – her mother could only say: 'That's all we need!' Later she had constant menstruation-related problems, which is common in women with an originally negative mother complex.

'The world is cold' – survival strategies

Those who have an originally negative mother complex are convinced that both they and the world are bad. It would be better not to exist. This feeling of primal guilt[100] has deep roots. That is why therapies which allocate blame and guilt can be accepted by such people, even though the guilt may be unjustified. A child who feels no right to exist, and who believes that it is his or her own fault, will – as long as enough vitality has been preserved – do everything in his or her power to attain this right. What strategies will such a person use?

Helma had an older sister who suffered from a variety of fears. She didn't dare approach anyone she didn't know. She kept her fears in check by means of compulsive behaviour: in particular a compulsion to collect things. She used to take many things from her younger brothers and sisters and knew how to keep hold of them once she had them. She was the focus for a great deal of aggression. Another way she had of attaining some some sort of self-esteem was by helping her mother with the little ones, who kept being born. She married young and had several children, though not as many as her mother, and died of cancer at the age of 38. Helma, on the other hand, found another way of dealing with her anxiety; she behaved as though she was afraid of nothing. In such a case, the anxiety remains but is suppressed and surfaces instead in the body. Despite self-assertive behaviour, deep physical tensions remain to plague us. At a young age, Helma developed a remarkable degree of independence, a forced, practical sort of autonomy. She also made herself useful to her mother. She would go and register the births of the new children. Later on she discussed her younger brothers' and sisters' progress with their teachers and dealt with the bank and with correspondence from the council. In other words she partially adopted the role of father. She is still good at taking care of practical matters. This capacity is of real value, even if it originally developed under enormous strain and pressure. It would be therapeutically disastrous to undermine such survival strategies.

Even in the very worst scenarios there are oases which make life possible. And people who have been least 'spoiled' are particularly able to seek them out and enjoy them. Helma relates that her mother, who was usually unapproachable and shut off in her own world, used to play the piano. When she did so, the whole atmosphere changed. 'Each time she played it seemed like Christmas.' So music became an important oasis in Helma's life. At the age of 12 she passed an audition to join a world-famous youth orchestra. A class-mate had told her about it, and she had organized her own application. To begin with her mother was quite against the idea: 'If you want to look ridiculous in front of everyone, then go and audition!' But Helma went nevertheless, was accepted and travelled with this orchestra round the world. 'At last there was somewhere where I was wanted and needed.' For the first time in her life she had a feeling of belonging, of a right to existence. Of course this situation led to a radical re-evaluation of her own worth. She played in front of her younger brothers and sisters who also, one by one, joined the orchestra, and for her mother. But it all became a bit much for her. People with an originally negative mother complex can justify their right to exist by mothering other people, by giving others what they never received themselves. That isn't a bad stategy either, for at least some kind of mothering comes into play. There is a danger, though, that they can easily exhaust themselves because they haven't developed a feeling for their own capacities. They constantly feel a need to justify their existence, but are almost never satisfied by the feedback they receive, and so endlessly continue to seek for that elusive self-esteem.

At the age of 21 Helma had to leave the youth orchestra. She began her studies – and suffered a breakdown. Without the orchestra she had no identity. Her breakdown expressed itself in all kinds of physical symptoms: infections, inflammations of the kidneys, sinus problems and uncontrollable diarrhoea. She was treated in a clinic which dealt with psychosomatic illnesses and subsequently sought help from psychotherapy. But despite all the therapy she continued to suppress her fear. At the age of

40 she again sought psychoanalytical help and was at last able to admit how much fear ruled her life, and to see how important accepting this fear was for her sense of identity. 'Since I have owned my fear I feel that I have a body.' By relinquishing the compensatory self-preservation strategies she had held onto for half a lifetime, she was able to deepen her understanding of herself and the way her childhood had formed and affected her.

Although things had improved for Helma from the age of 30 onwards, when she at least had a job and therefore some place in the world, she still felt inwardly isolated, 'like someone who wears a suit of armour. You have to wear it, because life is cold and stays cold. I just got used to it.' It was not until she was 42 that she learned you could fetch a hot water bottle or an extra blanket if you felt cold at night. A colleague of hers had suggested this – she wouldn't have thought of it herself. She is sure that you have to earn love, and that even then it is unlikely to come your way.

'You never manage to belong, whatever you do.' The demands which people with an originally negative mother complex make of themselves are unattainable. They will never feel they are worth loving, unlike those with an originally positive father complex who believe that love is within their reach. Although Helma felt inwardly worthless, she still attempted to make herself useful to others. She believed, at least, that she had a lot to offer other people; but those she tried to help felt she 'wanted too much from them'. In other words they sensed that she wasn't mothering them for their own sake, but to justify her own existence.

Helma had very little connection with her own body, but she always dressed very aesthetically. She felt that her life – and therefore also her body – were so shameful that she should hide herself away under beautiful clothes. She had many sexual encounters but few relationships that lasted for any length of time. The effect of her sexual abuse in childhood was not to make her turn away from men, but to give them whatever they wanted. She also needed to feel normal and believed that sexuality made her so. And such encounters gave her perhaps at least a little of the warmth and interest she so desperately missed. She also became gradually aware that she very much enjoyed seducing and having power over men; but she had no real pleasure in sex itself.

She is still very good at surviving and likes to help others profit from this ability as long as they 'are honest and mean well'. She is still affected by the complex-formula: 'Don't believe that people say what they really think of you.' Helma can't put her finger on why 'honest and well-meaning' is so important for her. After prolonged therapy she defines it more precisely as a sense that another person has 'taken her on' emotionally.

Many people find Helma 'distrustful'. She tries to control what happens around her; she will often enquire what exactly one means by a certain phrase or comment. She herself doesn't see this as distrust but as a realistic way of tackling life. It is natural, given her complex-background, that she very much needs to be in control of anything that might affect her. She has a very distant, cool relationship with her actual mother, unlike many other women with an originally negative mother complex, who often remain very tied to their mothers; they will let themselves be tyrannized and played upon in the hope of receiving, finally, their mother's approval and blessing. Helma holds out no such hope.

How can a woman with such a severely negative mother complex and such an ambivalent father complex survive? Helma developed an enforced independence to justify her existence, and this enabled her to draw from the oasis of music a new, encouraging perspective on her life. When the compensatory possibilities of this were exhausted, she was thrown back upon herself and again experienced all that she lacked. She entered therapy, in which she confronted her own past for the first time and began to feel a certain empathy with her situation – and could therefore find access to real aspects of herself.

Another oasis in Helma's childhood was provided by literature. She read a good deal, although her mother disapproved: 'You're always reading, why don't you *do* something!' She most liked reading biographies with happy endings, which enabled her to imagine alternative, happier realities. This helped her to keep alive some hidden hope of a better life. She sought access to the 'father-world' and assured herself a place in it through her studies. She was very gifted but still had to make an 'enormous effort' in order to feel her existence was justified.

Overstretched mothers

How a negative mother complex comes about

The originally negative mother complex is caused not only by the interaction between a child and mother, but also by the whole 'mother-realm'. Mothers who neither wanted children nor find they can relate to them offer the child little chance of a positive interaction. Mothers who are overstretched, perhaps because they are not supported by their partners, or because their partners unconsciously devalue their role, are often unsympathetic towards their children. Overdemanding mothers, who are more aware of themselves and their own wishes, find it very difficult to let their child develop in accordance with his or her own needs. Women with an originally negative mother complex from which they have not been able to emancipate themselves cannot easily show the child genuine interest. An originally negative mother complex can also arise when the parent and child are genuinely incompatible – which does occur. This is especially difficult in single-parent families, in which the complex will therefore become more and more impacted, resulting in a kind of mutual allergy. We must also remember how difficult it still is for a woman to find her real identity. When she becomes a mother she is suddenly meant to develop an assured, positive, motherly identity. A woman with a relatively positive mother complex can do this. But something seems wrong with a society which undermines feminine values in various ways, yet still expects a woman to step without difficulty into an ideal-mother identity.

CHAPTER 10

'As though paralysed'

The originally negative mother complex in men

Most men with this form of complex take refuge in a world of career and achievement in which they make strenuous demands on themselves. Since this world is still, today, a male domain, such men don't have quite such a hard time of it – especially if they are talented and can achieve some success – as women with a negative mother complex, who are faced with a severe identity problem if they try to derive their sense of self from the father-realm.

From stomach-aches to mortal fear – Helmut

A 46-year-old man – Helmut – sought therapy because of heart-related anxiety symptoms. He recalls a recurring image from his childhood: his mother is crying as she looks out of the window. It's snowing outside. Helmut thinks he's broken something and that he is guilty of causing his mother's tears. Perhaps that is why he can't run and comfort her. He feels paralysed. He thinks that this experience dates from the age of three or four – but similar situations arose often throughout his childhood. Later on he had still stronger feelings that he ought to say something to his mother, should perhaps also touch her; but his generalized, pervasive feeling of guilt always prevented him from approaching his mother. Both of them were very unhappy about it, he says.

Another image: 'It must have been shortly before I first went to school. I have a stomach-ache, as I often did – but this time it's really bad. My mother stands beside my bed and keeps repeating: "If only there was something I could do to help." I feel completely helpless, as well as agonizingly guilty that I'm causing her problems.' Another image: 'I'm sitting for hours on the toilet. I know that I can't rejoin the others before I've "done something".' The others had left him alone, excluded him because of his digestive problems. He is aware of his loneliness, his stomach-ache, his inability to produce what is required. And another image: his sister is playing – she's never any problem. She eats well. She's always dressed in white. He loved and looked up to his sister, but she always seemed rather remote. She was three years older than him and much less problematic.

Helmut was never allowed to disturb his father, who worked very hard. He can hardly ever remember his father speaking to him when he was young. He had a sense of being quite alone with his mother, plagued by his inability to comfort her, and by his physical problems. His sister was a shining – but not very real – star on the periphery of his existence. Later he realized that his absent father was desperately trying to keep his small business afloat. On his first day at school, his father said to him: 'Hopefully you'll be a bit more robust now you've got something to do.' Helmut didn't understand the word 'robust' but didn't dare to ask what it meant. A few weeks later he asked his teacher, then realized that his father's phrase contained both an implicit criticism and a small window of hope. But his overriding impression was one of astonishment that his father had actually addressed him directly.

Helmut describes his mother as a loving, but unselfconfident and depressive woman, who lived for her children. His sister seems to be a normal, self-assured woman, without any psychosomatic problems.

His mother later told him that he had had stomach problems even as a baby, and that no cure could be found in spite of consulting doctors and nurses. She had felt completely incapable of helping him. This feeling seemed to go hand in hand with periods of depression, which also drew her son into a vicious circle of helplessness. Both of them became convinced that no-one can doing anything for anyone else, especially when some-one feels ill. Helmut's needs were not answered, even though it is quite possible that his mother was more concerned about him than anyone else. He did not develop a sense of having an unquestioned right to existence. From an early age he had to pay for his stomach-aches by trying to cheer up his mother – evidently an impossible task. His father was busy and unavailable and, even if he had been more present, might well have only been disappointed in this son who was not 'robust' enough. Helmut was an excellent pupil, but his father always used to say only: 'At least you're good at school.' Helmut, focusing on the words 'at least', was sad, for he would have liked his father to be pleased with him.

This feeling of sorrow – the prevailing one for at least the first ten years of his life – still, today, underlies his attitude to the world: 'For as long as I can remember I've had a knot and pain in my stomach. That makes me feel I can't trust life, that everything is painful. Whether the pain is physical or emotional doesn't make any difference – it still hurts.' As a boy he felt more and more guilty about his mother's depression, believing that he had bitterly disapppointed her. He says that he still has to be careful not to feel responsible and guilty if he has dealings with depressed people. It was not until Helmut was 25 and had married a woman who had to be regularly hospitalized for fits of depression that his mother at last comforted him. She told him then that she herself had suffered from severe depressions, but that this had improved as she grew older. If she or Helmut's father had told him this much earlier, they might have saved the growing boy from some of the feelings of guilt and despair that plagued him.

As a child, Helmut himself was not really 'seen', although his mother compulsively observed his every movement. He can remember his temperature charts that she recorded for three years. He wasn't allowed out unless the weather was very mild. This made him feel different from the other children, an outsider. The members of his family had little emotional connection with one another. Instead of an 'oceanic' feeling of unity, Helmut had knots in his stomach and diarrhoea. Both his mother and father had also shown him that it was important to keep every situation under control.

In this complex there were also oases: Helmut was an excellent pupil, he enjoyed reading – mainly adventure novels – and was very good at imagining and creating three-dimensional structures. He remembers that his grandfather, at least, praised him for this. His relationship with his sister was also something of a positive influence: he looked up to her and wanted to please her, and secretly envied her.

The oasis of school was not wholly unproblematic. Because his mother molly-coddled him, his class-mates teased and taunted him. He therefore took refuge in his school work and began to develop rather obsessive patterns of behaviour, copying out his essays again and again until there wasn't a single mistake; or getting into a panic and making more and more mistakes because he was tired. He completed his studies successfully and did extremely well in his chosen career.

As already mentioned, he married a woman who later turned out to be depressive. He had three children with her, two sons and a daughter, with whom he has a good, warm relationship. Everything seemed to be going well; he found he was able to cheer up his wife when she felt down. Because he was reliable and steady she felt more secure with him than ever before, and he felt much less helpless with her than he had done with his mother. But then he met a woman who found him attractive. He reacted to this situation by putting all his energy into his work for several weeks. He tried to suppress the temptation which he had 'luckily escaped'. In line with his obsessive tendencies he took refuge in more control and order. But this worked only for a few months; then more and more 'temptations' presented themselves to him – women who showed an interest in him – and he started to have 'erotic fantasies'.

If we look at this situation not just as a 'disturbance', but also as an expression of a developmental process, of life itself calling to him, then we can see these temptations as the awakening of a new anima quality in his psyche which he projects onto 'seductresses' – an anima quality which might, to begin with, bring about sexual and erotic passion. This anima seems to be rather more open-ended than the image he projected onto his sister, and to stimulate qualities and aspects which he probably does not gain from his wife.

Helmut reacted to these intensifying temptation situations with a neurotically-based heart complaint. He became terrified of having a heart attack and dying, and therefore consulted a number of doctors.

He suffered the first anxiety attack on a Sunday morning, when trying to decide whether to stay at home with his wife or go to play golf. He knew that one of the 'temptresses' was waiting to meet him there. Suddenly his heart began to beat very fast and loud, he felt overwhelmed, oppressed, breathless; he was sweating like anything and was sure that his heart was going to stop and he would die. The emergency doctor was called.

Behind these neurotic symptoms lies a fear of separation. Helmut had never really emancipated himself. His unselfconfident mother had held onto him too long, not in an 'abundant' symbiosis, but in one which demanded an anxious retreat from the world into order and control, and provoked a projection of all that was frightening onto the body – which continually had to be observed. This sort of constricting, over-protective symbiosis, which anxiously tries to exclude what is bad but therefore also excludes the world and sees it as dangerous and threatening, hardly encourages a child to develop independence. In addition, the mother-image of the mother complex was here transferred fairly seamlessly onto the wife, and therefore no real separation took place. Erotic temptations in this situation are clearly an impetus towards separation; they lead out into the unknown and are also 'beyond the pale', since they are frowned on by society. Losing one's grip on an habitual and controlled pattern of life can be experienced as mortal fear, in this case projected onto a possible heart-attack. There is a further significance in all this, for if Helmut succumbed to the temptations, he would change. In other words, the old Helmut would indeed be 'dead'.

Helmut seemed like a depressive person who manages his depressions with very socially acceptable, very controlled, almost obsessive behaviour patterns. What he really longed for was the originally positive mother complex. He said: 'However much I try, I never feel really alive. The abundance I desire simply doesn't exist.'

Primal fear and distrust

Conclusions about the originally negative mother complex

People with an originally negative mother complex have in common the feeling that both they and the world are bad. They have no sense of an unquestioned right to existence, and they believe that they themselves are ultimately to blame for everything. It is also common for them to remain very attached, almost 'glued' to their mother or to people on whom they project the mother complex, even when their desires continue to be thwarted. They keep hoping, unconsciously, that the mother will at last 'give them her blessing' and realize she was wrong to undervalue them. Such people never really feel a sense of belonging to others, even though they strive for it with all their might. Inherent in their complex is a belief and expectation that they will always be rejected and treated badly. Their isolated ego has great difficulty in forming satisfactory relationships with other people. They are ruled by primal fear and distrust, which leads them to try to control everything as much as possible. This compensatory behaviour is often seen from the outside as a 'power complex', but it is in fact a desperate attempt to survive by someone who feels quite powerless. Their

primal distrust, as well as the capacity they developed in childhood for being over-aware of every situation – so as to avoid
dangerous situations or take advantage of more favourable
ones, means that they perceive the slightest emotional nuance
in the people around them; also that they very often interpret,
or misinterpret, such nuances as rejection. They will then
frequently react with great rage, which at least opens them up
emotionally and releases the life and energy within them, or
with repressed rage, with passive aggression. People suffering
from this complex have often not learned to deal properly wth
anger and aggression.

A feeling of hopelessness is inherent in their primal distrust.
Instead of a natural, unassailable unity with the world and other
people, the predominating sense of isolation and rejection
makes them struggle like anything to belong. Their capacity for
rivalry and jealousy is usually far stronger than their capacity for
active love, even though they will often make great demands
upon themselves in a relationship situation. Their enormous
longing to trust life and be part of it cannot be realized. Those
who have more vitality and greater access to helpful oases
within the complex may have the conviction that they must
struggle to make up for what is missing in their lives, whereas
those with less energy and fewer oases will continually accuse
the world of not providing what they need. But neither of these
approaches will really replace the feelings of love, acceptance
and self-esteem that they long for. Such people often seek
compensation through the father complex; they try to attain
self-esteem and social acceptance by means of their outer
achievements.

One invariably finds an originally negative mother complex,
combined with a weak father complex, underlying so-called
narcissistic disorders.[101] This not only severely threatens self-
esteem and causes many forms of related anxiety, but also
frequently brings about physical problems of a psychosomatic
nature.

Those who suffer from this complex will very often be in need
of therapy. If they can manage to gain insight into their close

identification with the image of a mother who does not accept them, if they can understand the extent to which they adopt this role in their relationships with other people, then they can use aggression to attack the destructive tendencies in themselves. Through such a process they can develop a capacity for enormous gratitude towards those who show them affection, or simply towards the world's rich abundance which they now sense. But it is a long, hard road to get so far. People with this form of complex have a primal, generalized feeling of guilt; it is therefore very hard for them to recognize, accept and battle against their problematic identification with a rejecting mother. This is usually only possible if a therapist can succeed in communicating empathy with the very difficult situation they found themselves in as children, and make them realize that they themselves were not to blame. Only then can one find out to what extent their actions are conditioned by their identification with the mother-aspect of their mother complex, or whether they are projecting the mother-image onto the world and other people. It is very important that they should feel the therapist has a genuine interest in them. Also, they should be encouraged to express all sorts of feelings, so as to find out who they really are and where their true gifts lie. It is essential that the value of the survival strategies they have developed is recognized and affirmed and not seen only as compensatory behaviour. It can be helpful to them to become aware of the 'oases' and other complexes they can draw on apart from the negative mother complex, since they have a strong tendency to see everything – themselves and the whole of life – in very bleak terms.[102]

Such a person would benefit from developing positive relationships with women and allowing different images of woman to arise in their psyche. But it is likely that this path will be closed to them, at least initially, since they expect only negative responses from women. Whether it becomes possible or not will depend partly on whether there have been childhood interactions with women other than the mother, which allowed more positive, motherly complex-patterns to come into play. If this has been the case, some residual hope will remain of a different model of oneself and the world, even if this is largely based 'only' on fantasy or literature. In the human psyche there are self-regulating forces at work; fantasies and archetypal images of a nurturing mother can help to heal a negative complex-pattern. It is also essential that such people do not try to find justification for their existence from other people. They have to acknowledge that this must ultimately come from themselves.

CHAPTER 11

The originally negative father complex in men

'Made to feel like nothing'

In what follows I will refer extensively to Franz Kafka's *Letter to My Father*,[103] which gives wonderful expression to the negative father complex as found in men. He wrote it at the age of 35, 5 years before his death, when his creative output was at its zenith. One of his many attempts to marry had again just come to nothing. This letter was probably written in an effort to emancipate himself from his father, since he had not managed to achieve this emancipation through marriage.

Letter to my father – Franz Kafka

We were so different from one another, and in such a way as to be so dangerous to each other; if anyone had thought of trying to predict how I, the slowly developing child, and you, the grown man, would behave towards each other, they might well have assumed that you would simply crush and obliterate me. But that didn't happen – life can't be worked out in advance – yet maybe what actually happened is still worse. I ask you, though, never to forget that I do not for a moment believe it was your fault. It was not in your power to influence me differently from the way you did. But you must stop thinking that I simply succumbed to this influence out of sheer spite.[104]

This passage characterizes the complex-atmosphere: the small boy's feeling that he may at any moment be crushed by the imposing father – in other words, that his right to exist is wholly dependent on the father and can be extinguished at any time. What has happened that is 'still worse'? This means, no doubt, that living with the fear of being crushed is worse than it actually happening. But before he goes into more detail, he tries to placate his father: he does not blame him; nor does he wish to carry the blame himself. He makes a reconciliatory gesture in the face of a most painful experience. Kafka then describes what one could call a complex-memory:

> From my earliest years I have only one specific memory. You may also remember it. It was night-time and I was whining for a drink of water – I probably wasn't thirsty but was partly doing it to be annoying, partly to get some attention. You told me off severely several times, but it had no effect. Then you took me from my bed, carried me out onto the veranda and left me standing alone there for a while in front of the closed door, in my night-shirt. I'm not saying that this was wrong – perhaps it was really the only way to get some peace; I'm just trying to describe the effect upon me of the methods you used in my upbringing. I'm sure I was obedient afterwards – but I suffered an inner hurt. I just couldn't understand that what I thought was quite natural behaviour – my pointless demand for water – should be met by this most terrible response. Years later I still suffered from the agonizing thought that my father, this enormous man, the ultimate authority, could, almost without any reason, come in the night and carry me from my bed out onto the veranda; and that therefore I meant nothing to him.
>
> That was not so important in itself, an intimation only. But the feeling I often have of being worth nothing stems largely from your influence. A little encouragement, a little friendliness, a little smoothing of my way is what I would have needed; instead you threw me off course, no doubt with good intentions since you wished me to follow a different path – but it was one I was not fit for.[105]

This memory, which may well be representative of many others that Kafka had of his father, forms a telling focus of his father complex. The little boy who dares to disturb the quiet, who is making himself and his needs known, is rejected by being put outside the door in his night-shirt. The child cannot understand why his behaviour has merited this disproportionate reaction. This results in the boy feeling that his father is an 'ultimate authority' with the power to reduce him to nothing at any moment, or at least to expose him to a deep and overpowering sense of shame. Kafka also makes clear that this kind of complex-experience has been repeatedly called forth through the years; also that he has projected it onto everything of a fatherly nature, including 'God the Father': he struggles continually with the idea that some ultimate authority may reduce him to a state of isolation, shame and worthlessness. What he would have needed instead, he says, is encouragement, friendliness, an openness to his needs.

A striking aspect of the son's negative father complex is that the father, by upholding his rules and laws, destroys the son's self-esteem. Unless the son can rebel – in which case he must forego his father's blessing – he will, in extreme circumstances, be made to feel shameful, guilty and worthless. The continual reprimands and punishment meted out to him make him feel that he must be guilty of some crime. The fact that he doesn't understand why he is at fault makes the guilt all the more agonizing and pervasive. As a result he will try in vain – though he doesn't perceive the hopelessness of his attempts – to satisfy the 'ultimate authority'. He becomes easy to manipulate. Kafka found it particularly distressing to observe that his father did not need to abide by the rules which he imposed upon his son.

> I wasn't allowed to crunch chicken-bones at a meal; but you were. I wasn't to slurp up vinegar; but you did. It was drummed into me that I should cut the bread in a very straight slice; but it was fine for you to do it with a knife dripping with sauce. No bits of food should fall on the ground; but under your chair lay the most remains. At table one was only to eat – nothing else; but you cleaned and cut your finger-nails, sharpened pencils, cleaned your ears with a tooth-pick. Please understand, Father: these were, in themselves, quite insignificant matters; what made them distressing

was the fact that you yourself – a person whose enormous authority I looked up to – did not observe the very rules which you imposed upon me. This split my world into three realms: one, in which I lived like a slave subjected to laws invented for me alone, unable, for some reason I could never understand, to comply with them adequately; a second, infinitely far removed from mine, in which you lived, from which you dispensed rules and grew angry when they were not adhered to; and a third, where all other people lived happily, free of orders and obedience.[106]

The father, whose decrees are absolute, invents rules which apply only to the son. The son is thereby elevated to a special position; but he pays dearly for it, since he becomes a slave of the rules which he can never wholly satisfy. The son is therefore rejected and isolated, banished to a world separate from that of his father, convinced of his inadequacy to satisfy the father-world's demands. He also develops a fantasy that all other people are free, untroubled by rules and orders.

A second aspect of the negative father complex is that the son, rather than being encouraged to go his own way, has to follow the path mapped out for him by his father. This may not be so bad if a father at least perceives what his son is really like. But the more a father is aware only of himself, and the less he can recognize his son's real qualities, the more damaging is his apparent 'care and concern'.

A third aspect of the negative father complex – and for me the most telling of all – consists in the fact that a son is unable either to form a mutual, good, 'us-relationship' with his father, or to identify with him at all. This is expressed in another passage of Kafka's letter:

I needed encouragement more than anything – how I needed it! I was already overwhelmed by your physical presence alone. I remember, for instance, how we used to get undressed together in a changing cubicle. I was thin, measly, weak; you were strong, broad, big. I felt pitiful, not only in front of you, but in front of the whole world as well, for you were the standard I measured everything against. But it was even worse when we came out of the cubicle in front of other people: I, like a small skeleton holding your hand, unsure, bare-footed, frightened of the water, incapable of managing the swimming motions you kept showing me with good intentions, but nevertheless to my deep embarrassment. At such times all my worst experiences surfaced and united to reduce me to complete despair.[107]

A boy's 'us-experience' will usually be confirmed and supported by undressing with his father and holding his hand when they are among other people. The physical presence of an adult is not experienced as threatening if a complex is sufficiently positive; the child identifies with it, or at least makes it his future ideal. But Kafka compares himself unfavourably with his father, feeling that he ought to be like him, and therefore believing himself to be worthless. It is the same when his father tries to show him how to swim – which ought to be a positive, affirming experience. Instead, he feels alone. He has also already internalized his over-demanding father's requirements of him – typical of an originally negative father complex. He experiences his father as unfeeling, as a dominating figure who ruthlessly exercises his power:

> I couldn't understand that you had no feeling for the suffering and shame your judgemental words could cause me; it was as if you had no inkling of your power . . . you kept on battering me with your phrases. You were never sorry for anyone, neither then nor later; against you everyone was quite defenceless.

The son has enormous demands laid upon him, as is characteristic of the negative father complex:

> I was always in disgrace. Either I followed your commands; that was a disgrace for they were intended for me alone. Or I was disobedient; that was also a disgrace, for how could I dare to be disobedient to you? Or I couldn't carry out your commands because I didn't have your strength, or appetite, or ability – although you expected and demanded that I should have; that was the greatest disgrace of all.[108]

It is disgrace to submit to his father because it means that he is unable to define his own rules. It is disgrace also to rebel because it is forbidden by his father. ('Don't let me hear one word of disagreement!'[109]) He is trapped in a web of contradiction which prevents him from discovering his own impulses. The fact that he feels dwarfed and overwhelmed by his father's strength, appetite and ability tells us that the father probably needed to feel superior to the son. Also that the son was unable to distance himself from these ridiculous demands. It is typical of the originally negative father complex that one must uphold authority or else feel worthless. The only way of defending oneself against the 'ultimate authority' is to become like this authority oneself. This doesn't bring real freedom though. Such people demand too much of themselves and therefore inevitably fail to achieve their unattainable goals – and then, once more, feel destroyed. Underlying the demands imposed upon oneself is the desire to be like the father and so create an 'us-experience' which will invoke the father's blessing. The more the son has the feeling of not being how his father wanted, the stronger will be this desire.

In the originally negative father complex, the dominance of the father is part and parcel of the suppression of the son, whose trust in himself is undermined. He is rejected as a self-determining human being; to be accepted he must deny himself to please the father – definitely a no-win situation. In this complicated, over-demanding position, Kafka became speechless:

> Your threat: 'No word of disagreement!' and your hand raised to emphasize this phrase, have accompanied me ever since. In your presence I . . . started to speak in a halting, stuttering way; that didn't please you either. In the end I kept my mouth shut, to begin with perhaps in defiance, but then because I could neither think nor speak in your presence.[110]

To withdraw into silence is a way of protecting oneself – at least temporarily – from an impossible situation; yet it also leads one deeper into isolation.

Another means of escaping would be to form contacts with other people. Kafka tried this, but it was also sabotaged:

Because of how I was, I only occasionally showed some interest in another person. But whenever I did, without any consideration for my feelings or judgement, you would let loose a barrage of attack and slander.[111]

Obviously it was forbidden to think well of another person. That might have led to a situation in which the father was no longer the absolute measure of all things. It would also, of course, have been the first step towards self-emancipation.

Another way of escape was to do battle with his father by using his own methods, taking on shadow aspects in the process:

To assert myself a little at least, and partly from a desire for a kind of revenge, I soon began to make a note of various mannerisms of yours which struck me as silly; I 'collected' them and exaggerated them. For example, the way you let yourself be over-awed by people who seemed to occupy a higher station than yourself, and kept telling of your encounters with them – a councillor of the Kaiser, say, or other such people . . . or I observed your prediliction for rude and loudly uttered turns of phrase, which made you laugh as though you had said something particularly clever, although it was really just some humdrum little obscenity. (At the same time, though, it was also a further expression of your vitality, which shamed me.) Of course there were plenty of such things to notice, and I took pleasure in them . . . for me they were a means – an insufficient one though – of retaining my self-respect; they were jests such as are made at the expense of gods and kings – jests which not only go hand in hand with the deepest respect, but also actually belong to it.[112]

To clearly perceive his father's weaknesses was a way of separating himself and retaining some control over his own life. But it was still, as Kafka says, 'insufficient'; in spite of the foibles and failings Kafka perceived, his father remained godlike for him.

We may ask what role his mother played in his conflict with his father and the father complex. Understandably, since it is a letter to his father, little mention is made of his mother. She seems to have made herself subordinate to her husband, whom she loved. Apparently she tried to balance out his toughness with her gentleness.[113]

> If I wanted to escape from you I had also to flee from the family itself, even from my mother. I could always run to her for protection, but not from you. She loved you too much, was too faithful to you to have stood up against you for very long on behalf of her child.[114]

The son had no real help from his mother because she was not an independent person. Her example showed him that it was better to comply with the father than to try to flee his influence:

> Unconsciously my mother took on the role of a 'beater' at the hunt. If ever, by some faint chance, your method of bringing me up could have set me on my own feet through the defiance, disinclination or even hatred that it caused, my mother brought me back into the fold with her kindness, her reasonable approach (in the chaos of my childhood she was the picture of reason itself) and her intercession on your behalf. If it had not been for this I might have broken free from the sphere of your influence – to the advantage of us both.[115]

The image which Kafka chooses is a striking one: his mother is a beater in the hunt who drives him, the wild animal, into the path of the hunter, his father. The idea, though, that he might have freed himself from his father through defiance or hate, if his mother had not been so gentle and mediating, seems to me very hypothetical. This doesn't alter the fact that the son felt trapped. A proper confrontation with the father was obviously not possible:

> There was no real conflict between us; I was soon overpowered. All that remained for me was flight, bitterness, sadness and inner conflict.[116]

Entangled in a negative self-image

The difficulties of freeing oneself from this complex

Writing was an important oasis within this pervasive complex:

> Your dislike of my habit of writing was more well founded.

Unbeknown to you it had helped me free myself from you a little –
though only perhaps as much as a worm whose rear end is caught
under someone's foot and, tearing its front end free, drags itself to
one side. When I wrote, I felt a little more secure; I could breathe a
bit. The annoyance you naturally showed at my writing was, unusually, welcome to me. My vanity and ambition, it is true, suffered
rather from the way you greeted my books: 'Leave it on the table!'
(you were usually playing cards when one of my books came)
but basically I had a good feeling about your reaction; not only
from consuming malice or from pleasure at having my view of our
relationship confirmed, but primarily because your phrase sounded
to me like my freedom, my release. That was of course an illusion. I
was not free; and would not be so without much good fortune. You
were the object of my writing. It gave me a vehicle for complaining
of all those things I could never speak to you directly about. It was
an intentionally long draw-out farewell from you, forced upon me
by you, it is true, but nevertheless given impetus and direction by
myself.[117]

Kafka used his writing for the purpose of his emancipation; as
such it played a more decisive part in his achievement of autonomy than is suggested by the worm image. Writing was a realm
unoccupied by the father, in which, therefore, the son had a
degree of freedom to structure things in his own way. The
expression, in his writing, of his obsession with the father complex world, would certainly have been a means for separating
himself from it; it is not clear, though, whether he really
achieved this. We can see from his work how such a one-sided
complex can heighten sensitivity towards manifestations of this
same complex in society at large. But it is also apparent that
Kafka strongly internalized his originally negative father complex. He judged his writing as harshly as his father would have
done, even though he recognized its intrinsic value in helping
him assert his identity. We can perceive two extremes of the
father complex at work in him, although he himself was mostly
aware of one – the 'worm' which could find a refuge through
creativity. He could still not really take pleasure in his success,
though, since he was denied his father's blessing and had
adopted his father's own opinion of himself.

My self-esteem was far more dependent on you than than on anything else, such as outward success.[118]

Writing was not enough to secure Kafka's 'release' from his
dominating father complex, so he tried to achieve it through
marriage:

Marriage certainly holds the promise of full self-emancipation and
independence. If I had a family I would have attained, in my view,
the most important thing of all – which is also the highest peak of
your own achievement. I would be on a level with you, all the old –
and constantly renewed – disgrace and tyranny would be a thing of
the past . . . Marriage is my highest aspiration, it would bring the
most honourable independence; but it is also, at the same time, so
closely connected with you . . . and is closed to me, because it is the
realm you have made your own.[119]

Kafka's attempts at marriage are doomed to failure; he cannot
embark on a marriage of which the ultimate aim is to enable
him to become his father's equal and so emancipate himself. A
fascination with female qualities, though, would have allowed
him to experience and integrate aspects of himself that were
not dominated by the patriarchal father complex.

In his very interesting foreword to the letter, Emrich draws
out the salient features of Kafka's problematic relationship with
his father:

Kafka's absolute, truth-seeking, male 'self' cannot see in his beloved
an absolute, truth-seeking, female 'self'. He is therefore denied a
love which could have broken the vicious circle of dominance and
subordination, of superiority and inferiority . . . [120]

Woman has no place in this father complex system. Love is
therefore not possible. Emrich is also of the opinion that Kafka
is not principally addressing the problems surrounding his relationship with his father in this letter, but that he is describing
the collapse of a patriarchal world. The 'Father-God' is shown
as one who suppresses his sons; their guilt and self-sacrifice
serve no purpose, and the absolute unity of father and son is

seen as one which cannot be attained. Women are not able, either, to contribute to this unity.

Of course the letter can also be taken in this way. Kafka's own negative father complex, which certainly caused him great personal suffering, is related to the nature of a patriarchal world. The particular patterns of suppression he was subjected to can also be found in more generalized social systems which have a similar destructive effect. Anyone who both suffers from a personal complex and has the creativity to express it will always also describe aspects of social and cultural life which resonate with their own problems.

We may well ask ourselves why it was that Kafka failed to emancipate himself to a greater degree. The whole letter is pervaded with a hunger for his father's acceptance and love. He desperately sought his father's blessing, could not accept that he would have to live without it. His fixation on the father complex may have been rooted in the fact that the two men really wished to love each other, but that this was not possible because they were so different. Kafka did make attempts to free himself. His creativity in particular would have been an excellent way to forge his separate identity, if his complex had not forced him to continually underrate and devalue his own work. Identification with the 'ultimate authority', the inner, judgemental patriarch, sabotages in advance any possibility of finding a way out of the maze. The only thing that can help is to show oneself some love and consideration. The mother can provide an example of this; but in Kafka's case, his mother was so interwoven with the father-world that every influence of hers was also undermined.

The main characteristics of the originally negative father complex in men

1 Fathers are seen as the representatives of a valid set of laws. In spite of all their efforts, the sons remain insignificant. Instead of solidarity – an 'us-relationship' – there is a master–servant pattern at work. Instead of participation and

involvement, the sons have a feeling of being manipulated by a stronger force, of being slaves. It is common for persecution complexes to develop.

2 It is forbidden to go one's own way. A son must follow the path his father has pre-ordained. Fantasies, which are invariably concerned with finding oneself, are taboo; instead, conformity is required – though the son's efforts in this direction are never sufficient.

3 The son strives to be on an equal level with the father, who is his rival – though this is not openly expressed. The son is not helped and encouraged, but asked why he can't yet manage to do something. The son has no pleasure in his achievements; he always lags several steps behind the father's demands. It seems he is being offered 'togetherness' with his father as a reward for his achievements; but this is an emotional carrot that is always out of reach. The son can never satisfy his father's demands. Instead he feels continual shame and guilt. Even if he should ever satisfy, or exceed the conditions and requirements laid upon him, he would still not receive recognition, for his father would simply set him a further 'impossible' task.

4 The overriding feeling of this complex pattern is one of shame and guilt, connected with feelings of insignificance. These often cause difficulties in speech or self-expression, as well as a desire for revenge and destruction. At a more advanced stage, the son will try to achieve equality with the father, so as to overcome his feelings of guilt and shame. The situation then becomes compounded with difficulty, since he is seeking recognition which will never be sufficiently available in the way he would like. As long as he continues to seek this recognition from a parental aspect of his complex, he will be trapped in a vicious circle. The only way through is to learn to forfeit this need for his father's acceptance. He must, instead, provide his own self-justification.

Men with an originally negative father complex have a great need for recognition from other men. If they get it, though, they will distrust and devalue it. Extreme rivalry also belongs to the negative father complex; it is actually indicative of the fact that the son's self-esteem has not been wholly crushed out of him. He will experience this rivalry as extremely painful, for in the depths of his soul he knows that he will be the loser. This is partly because he has internalized the critical father so that it has become an unconscious aspect of his ego complex; partly also because by coming out on top of a situation he would in fact destroy his chances of receiving the blessing of a father figure – which, against all reasoning, is what he really longs for. Such men also carry this self-critical, self-undermining attitude into their own relationships. They are as hard on others as they are on themselves, and can as little accept and recognize other people's achievements as they can their own. They make enormous, strenuous efforts whose results they can never enjoy.

To begin to deal with such a complex, one must become aware of its two opposed extremes. The internalized father aspect must become conscious so that one can keep it within firm bounds. Feelings such as 'Everyone else is a success, but I am nothing' must be traced back to their complex-origin and if possible revised – or even perhaps, for a while, forbidden to oneself.

The most important thing is to search for a path of one's own, without the father's blessing. To do this, the desire to be as successful as, or even more so than the father, must be sacrificed. If one can dissociate oneself from rivalry, then spheres of life become available which were not part of the father complex pattern. These are, above all, the realms of the anima.

CHAPTER 12

The originally negative father complex in women

'I'm no good for anything'

The originally negative father complex has various different effects upon women, depending on the kind of father figure we are dealing with.

'I already know that you'll never manage it' – Karin

Karin is a woman of 23 who has a high-level job in a bank. She is extremely well qualified and has already achieved much in her chosen career. But she feels constantly tired and low, and suffers from a variety of minor ailments. Her GP suggested consulting a psychotherapist; he felt that there was something wrong with her 'defence mechanisms' against infection, which might not have a merely physical cause.

She strikes me as energetic and capable, someone who knows what she wants; she walks with a brisk step and neither says too little nor too much. She cries very easily – but her crying has a somewhat forced quality: her face first contorts without any sound, then she utters a quiet, pained cry. It strikes one as though she is torn between the need to cry and the refusal to allow herself to. She is very quick to pass judgement on herself: 'I'm not really any good for anything – it's just that no-one's found out yet. I'm just not consistent enough for someone in a managerial position. I scrape by because I work harder than anyone else. What I lack in talent, I make up for in effort. That's what I was always told as a child, and it's true.'

Karin demands a great deal of herself. If she doesn't manage to come up to scratch in her own estimation, she feels herself to be worthless, without any identity. But even when she does satisfy her own criteria, she can't credit herself with having done a good job. Karin is also very tough and demanding towards other people; for instance, she endlessly criticizes her boss. Like her, other people are also 'worthless' if they don't make the grade. She doesn't look for excuses or mitigating factors – they can't be forgiven. 'I'm my father's daughter in that respect,' she says. She has a very critical eye; but her whole life is also exposed to the absolute, critical eye of God – an eye which for her is not in the least gentle or forgiving. She feels continually guilty. She remembers her father always saying to her: 'Some basic rules have simply to be respected – otherwise I cannot call you my daughter; but I know (and at this point he would sigh) that you won't manage it.'

She tries desperately to come up to his standards. She is utterly convinced that she will never manage it, yet simultaneously harbours the desperate hope that she will.

She too has some oases in her life: she is very gifted with her hands. Since the age of 18 she has spent her free time working with clay. Many people have suggested that she should have an exhibition of her beautiful, original pottery. Whenever she begins to organize this, she always ends up cancelling it. Her creations, she feels, could never stand up in front of the critical eyes of others.

She describes herself as 'very lonely emotionally. I belong to no-one, and never have.' A drawing which she did in her childhood shows, on one side, her parents and brothers and sisters. But she herself appears on the back – a clear demonstration that she did not feel part of the family, that, in fact, she had no experience of shared involvement whatsoever. She does not have any close relationships, only a working contact with her colleagues. She says that she has no time for such things, and anyway finds men and women of her age 'uninteresting'. When, occasionally, she goes to a social gathering of some kind, she invariably ends up on her own. Even at work she feels isolated and rejected – as she does now, in the therapeutic sessions with me. It is not until much later in the therapeutic process that she becomes aware of her own marked tendency to reject other people. At work her colleagues regarded her as occupying a moral and intellectual high ground. They felt themselves 'subjected to critical scrutiny whenever I'm around'.

'You'll never become a proper woman'

Background to this complex

Karin's mother always used to say: 'I'm keeping out of it, it's up to your father.' Karin was the eldest child; her parents were disappointed that she was a girl, for they had wanted someone to carry on the family name. Nevertheless, she was very close to her father, and remained so even when he eventually had a son. Her father was very strict about being moral and upright. At the age of six, she once stole 20p. Even when she was 14 and her father was still going on at her, saying 'Manners and decency are the most important thing in life – but you probably won't come up to scratch in that department,' she was convinced that he was still thinking of the bit of money she'd stolen; she didn't dare to ask though. Her father thought that exam results and academic achievement were very important; the fact that she was a high achiever at school helped her to 'keep my special place in my father's esteem'. Her father himself had not pursued his studies very far. He insisted that her excellent school-report, at the time she could have gone to grammar school, was in fact not good enough; and that she was therefore not cut out to be a grammar school pupil. He did not allow himself to be dissuaded by her teacher – she never went to grammar school. At the time she believed this decision showed that he took his 'fatherly duty' seriously. Only later did she bear a secret grudge against him for this. She tells me: 'He kept a continual watch on my homework, the books I read, the friends I had, the clothes I wore . . . I longed for him to say that he was proud of me; I still long for it.' But it then occurs to her that her father may be unable to accept her, since she has already achieved more than he did. She recalls that he always demanded she should be top of the class, but that he also always said that school marks were of no consequence in life. She, too, will have to do without her father's blessing.

She is able to redirect her desire for her father's recognition and live without it; but she would also like to be free of the pressure and compulsion to be appreciated by someone. She has come to understand that she projects this longing for appreciation upon many different people who take the place of her father, especially at work. Now she wants to just *be*. It is typical of a woman with a negative father complex that she *is* capable of doing without the appreciation of a father or multiple father figures. Her feminine self is not wholly identified with them, and therefore she does not totally lose her identity in the absence of their appreciation. Instead she is forced to seek her identity in realms which do not fall within their influence.

During this therapeutic process she began to feel a great rage towards her mother, who had 'simply left me in my father's clutches'. She came to the point of thinking that her mother had actually had her first child for the father's sake, had handed her over to him and then quietly got on with bringing up her other two children – who were both quite different from Karin – in peace. She and her mother, she felt, were also very different, probably always had been. But gradually images arise in her, mainly in dreams, of motherly women who provide her with security and comfort. She also begins to remember certain experiences of closeness with her mother which show that she was not simply 'handed over'.

Helen

A 26-year-old woman tells me of her disillusionment with her father: 'I was about 11 when my father first said that he doubted whether I'd ever become a proper woman. From then on he kept saying it. I tried to find out what he meant by a "proper woman". One day he pointed out to me a woman with a fine figure, well made-up, with a plunging neckline. When I was 13, he told me it was high time I developed some real curves; and yet again said I was unlikely to become a real woman. So I tried to dress up to please him. He was important to me – I wanted him to be pleased with me, even though it seemed beyond my powers. When I had the beginning of a bosom, I tried wearing a plunging neckline. Then he said to me: "You're becoming a whore." Whatever I did was wrong. Until I was 20, I kept trying everything I could think of to please him. But nothing worked. I tried the same thing with young men, but always had the feeling that I was not really seen. At last I found a woman who helped me discover myself as a woman. What I still can't understand is why I thought my father was all-important. My mother is OK. She always used to tell me I was fine, there was nothing wrong with me. But she was playing the same game as well, I suppose: she always tried to please my father, without success. To keep expressing disatisfaction with people around you has quite a powerful effect!

This form of father complex was directed towards a woman's outward appearance; it invoked the anxiety of having to accommodate oneself to a man in such a way as to lose one's identity, without gaining much in the process. This complex did not affect the realm of work and achievement, but influenced Helen's relationships with men.

Although neither woman was physically raped, their development as women was still violated. They were subjected to their father's will instead of determining their own paths and discovering the laws of their own nature. Both of them longed for acceptance and their father's blessing; but Helen, who had a much better relationship with her mother, could make do without this blessing far sooner than Karin. Neither of these daughters could establish an 'us-relationship' with their fathers. Their attempts to do this through achievement or conforming to expectations were doomed to failure. Their real identity was, however, not seriously threatened; their unrewarded struggle for recognition helped them to see, sooner or later, that there must be other ways to live. A desire awoke in them for real sharing. They sensed that their longing for an oceanic experience of life could not be satisfied by these fathers, who were so intent on preventing their daughters from growing up and outgrowing them.

Fathers who deny their daughters a real experience of sharing compel them to look beyond the father complex realm to find their own space and identity. Father complexes which less obviously circumscribe a daughter's search for identity can be more problematic. Such a woman may have a less obvious need for emancipation, but this may well cause her to remain stuck in a daughter role – for which she may be praised but ultimately not taken seriously enough. She may make great efforts to remain subordinate to her father, and in consequence to men in general. By 'keeping her head down' in this way, she will feel apologetic for herself, and somewhat guilty – but this will not provide a strong enough impetus to drive her forward in the active search for her real self.

CHAPTER 13

Staking out territory in the unknown

Conclusion

Very few people are subject to the influence of such extreme, one-sided complexes – to the detriment of the other parental complex – as are described in this book. What I have portrayed here should be seen as the basic elements of an approach to understanding each individual person's particular complex-patterns. There is no end to the possible variations and combinations of father and mother complexes. Yet even people whose mother and father complexes are in relative harmony will experience times in their lives when certain interactions or situations will draw from them a more one-sided complex-response. It is therefore less a question of asking oneself 'Do I have an originally positive mother complex?' than 'When do I experience it, when does it surface and how does it affect my self-image and my relationships?' Or 'When my father complex is activated, how does it show itself? Do I have to react in old, stereotyped ways, or can I find other ways of responding?'

In the absence of actual parents, the complex-process usually seeks out parent figures to replace them. If there is no father available, for instance, the father complex will be configured by interaction with other male figures. The positive side to this is that such a complex will be more multi-faceted, since it will have formed in reaction to many different men. It will also, though, be more susceptible to the archetypal images of father-liness prevailing at any particular time, to collective values and influences. This, in my opinion, makes emancipation harder; the closed, confining complex-patterns which normally give us an impetus for 'breaking out' are hardly present, and such people therefore do not feel the need for separation. It is actually much more difficult to free ourselves from fantasies we are hardly aware of than from actual parent figures. But it is of course also true that, even when a person who has had a formative effect on a complex-pattern of ours is still present and continues to interact with us, the complex will nevertheless contain a good deal of both personal and archetypal fantasy.

We also need to recognize that there are such things as 'collective complexes', which also influence us. In a society such as ours, in which male values are dominant and desirable, and values connected with the mother complex are therefore considered less important – are in fact unconsciously devalued – our personal complex-structure is embedded in a collective father complex. For women this is a negative complex in so far as it hinders them from seeking and determining their own indi-viduality. It may also, to some extent, affect men negatively, allowing them to remain as 'sons' rather than exploring their real potential. The mother complex-realm is apparently ideal-ized; but looking deeper, one finds that it is undermined and negated. This means that even a very positive mother complex contains the shadow of a collectively devalued mother complex. Even women, therefore, who feel comfortable in their female identity are continually confronted by collective doubt about their value. But we have begun to see a reaction against this: many women are now activated by a longing to determine their own female identity and assert its integrity and value.

Prepared to be reborn

We need to emancipate ourselves by separating from our parents at the right time. Many problems – in the social and political domain as well as the personal – are caused by a failure to achieve this separation. That does not mean that we should be able to free ourselves altogether from the influence of parental complexes. What is possible, though, is to confront those aspects of our psyche which time and time again throw up the same patterns and difficulties. It is especially important to recognize our unconscious identification with mother or father configurations. Our failure to emancipate ourselves from them will leave us at the continual mercy of fears and expectations which do not properly connect with reality. We may even invest much time and energy in complicated compensatory patterns, which ultimately leave us dissatisfied. We may well also be plagued by diffuse feelings of guilt – and rightly so, since we are not being ourselves, are not developing and delving ever further into the selves we could become, but hiding behind the 'protection' of our complexes. Not to realize oneself, one's potential, is something worth feeling guilty about; our unconscious will usually react to our avoiding tactics. Fromm's concept[121] is helpful here: he sees human life as a continuing process of birth, in which every stage is only transitory, and whose aim, ultimately, is 'to be born before we die'.

The readiness to be continually reborn is the same as continually questioning the habits which arise from the formative influence of our complexes. We must be prepared to renounce the ways of thinking and behaviour we are so used to, and which are therefore 'safe'. We need courage both to separate ourselves from others, and to open ourselves to them again. When we free ourselves from the influence of mother and father, we leave behind us a whole landscape, or at least transmute it into other forms. We have to stake out territory in the unknown – and for this we can rely only on our own feelings, thinking, dreaming, and capacity for going out towards others. We may well have to make a conscious decision to stick with our own thoughts and feelings even if we have no guarantee that they are 'right'. They will be more right for us than the thoughts and feelings of others.

It is not the aim of the emancipation process to eradicate all signs of the complex-patterns which have formed us, but to develop a sense for our own feelings in any situation, as opposed to those which arise out of the complex; we can recognize the latter by their habitual, repetitive nature. We need, above all, to be able – at least sometimes – to say 'I', and mean it, rather than resorting to a generalized, collective value-system.

If we can do this, then we can also recognize and relate to a 'you' in another person. We can open ourselves to another's abundance because we are not simply projecting aspects of our complexes onto them, and seeking either a pre-ordained fulfilment or confirmation of our poor expectations.

In the political arena, people who have freed themselves sufficiently from mother or father complexes will assume more real responsibility for themselves; they will not always wait for mother or father figures to act in order to criticize them immediately for their actions. I imagine that politicians might, if they had achieved sufficient emancipation, develop a greater sense of fellowship with each other, as brothers and sisters working towards shared aims, and might also more easily relinquish their role to others when it was called for. Emancipation is a hard road to travel; to take on responsibility for oneself is also hard. But what we gain is a feeling that we are living our own lives, a feeling of being real and of value. That in turn means that we have more energy for life and are altogether more interesting people.

Sharing or achievement – opposite principles

In conclusion I would like to examine the theme once more from a collective point of view.

Haerlin[122] distinguishes between a goal-orientated ego and one orientated towards sharing and participation. He believes that our contemporary problems are in large part due to our unbalanced emphasis on the 'achievement ego' at the expense of the 'participatory ego'. 'The dead-end in which our goal-orientated society is stuck has given rise to a longing for a more participatory consciousness.'[123] Included in goal-orientated processes is everything that we construct and create, as opposed to participation, which consists of all that is 'given',[124] such as our breathing, sleep and dreams – in which our ego participates but which it does not create.

The participatory ego has a basic sense of having the right to exist and therefore also to have a share in everything, to feel itself part of the world in the widest sense. The 'sharing' ego is therefore one which, in my terminology, is underpinned by the originally positive mother complex and can therefore open itself trustingly to life. The ego, on the other hand, which, according to Haerlin,[125] believes itself to be bad – and which I see as being influenced by an originally negative mother or father complex, has no such sense of a right to exist. 'If life is bad, achievement must make up for it.'[126] The feeling of not being worth-while continually compels a person to try to prove by his or her achievements that his or her existence is justified. Such achievement does not arise from pleasure in an activity but from inner compulsion; the achievement itself is not the important thing, but the self-justification it provides. That is also why the achievements of others must be matched against one's own and, where possible, denigrated so as to put oneself in a superior light. Strategies of all kinds are used to diminish the self-esteem of other people, which weakens the social coherence and energy of everyone. Haerlin draws the following conclusion: 'The crisis in the nature of our participative consciousness is also a crisis of the feminine, and of the world as seen by women. Achievement-consciousness has developed out of all that is motherless and unfeminine.'[127]

Haerlin thus diagnoses our world as one ruled by the father complex, one which offers little in the way of warmth and protection, since the realm of the mother complex has been so devalued; emancipation is demanded – but only from this feminine realm. It is the father complex world which has led to our desperate struggle to achieve at all costs, which hinders the development of our full humanity, and which causes a great deal of difficulty in our relationship to ourselves, each other and the world.

There exists, though, a collective longing for the realm of the positive mother complex, of participation, of 'anima'. This longing is particularly apparent among women. Such a realm is generally still devalued and considered 'dangerous, threatening, devouring, chaotic', etc. To the father complex world, in contrast, are attributed liberating, ordering, clarifying qualities. We must free ourselves from this dogma, which helps perpetuate the ruling systems in our society and also closes off whole realms of experience which are important for our health and well-being.

I hope I have been able to show that every form of complex carries within it certain problems as well as possibilities; and that the ego complex must repeatedly free itself from its particular formative circumstances through processes of separation and new conjunction.

Collective longing for the positive mother complex should be taken very seriously. It is not just some illusory desire for a lost paradise, but a longing for a manifold abundance of realms of life and feeling which are sorely needed.

Notes

Introduction

1 Jung, CW 9/1
2 Kast, 1992[1]
3 von Franz, 1970; Jacoby, 1985; Dieckmann, 1991
4 Rhode-Dachser, 1991
5 ibid

1 Loosening parental ties

6 Jung, CW 3
7 Blos, 1987
8 Rhode-Dachser, 1990
9 Blos, 1987
10 Freud, *The Interpretation of Dreams*, in Blos, 1987
11 *see also* Dieckmann
12 Rhode-Dachser, 1991
13 Rhode-Dachser, 1990
14 ibid
15 Kast, 1984
16 Kast 1992[3], 1991; Flaake/King, 1992
17 Kast, 1991
18 Hancock, 1930
19 Hagemann-White, in Flaake/King, 1993
20 Bernardoni/Werder, 1990
21 Kast, 1992[2]
22 Stern in Flaake/King, 1992
23 Kast, 1991
24 Scarr, 1987
25 Jung, CW 9/1
26 Rhode-Dachser, 1990
27 Flaake, 1989
28 Kast, 1992[2]

2 Complexes and episode memories

29 Kast, 1992[1]
30 Jung, CW 3, particularly: 'The Feeling-toned Complex and Its General Effects on the Psyche'
31 Stern, 1991
32 Tulving, 1972
33 Stern, 1991
34 Jung, CW 10
35 Stern, 1991
36 ibid
37 ibid
38 Kast, 1992[1]
39 Jung, 'A Review of the Complex Theory', in CW 8
40 ibid
41 ibid
42 *compare with* Kast, 1992[1]
43 Jung, 'The Associations of Normal Subjects', in CW 2
44 Jung, CW 8
45 Jung, 'The Ego', in CW 9/2

3 The originally positive mother complex in men

46 An expression coined by Peter Haerlin, 1987
47 von Franz, 1970
48 Kast in Pflüger, 1988
49 Hillmann, 1979
50 Fromm, 1989
51 For the practicalities and techniques of working on and with complexes, *see* Kast, 1992[1]

4 The originally positive mother complex in women

52 Chodorow, 1979
53 Kast, 1989
54 Kast, 1993[2]

5 Live and let live

55 *compare with* Kast, 1992[1]

56 Enke, 1991
57 Papousek
58 Erikson, 1994
59 Haerlin, 1987
60 Kast, 1984; *compare also with* Kast, 1993[2]
61 Jung, CW 9/2
62 Haerlin, 1987
63 Jung, CW 5
64 ibid, CW 10
65 ibid
66 Jung, CW 8; Kast, 1992[1]
67 Jung, CW 15
68 Kast in Rhode-Dachser, 1992
69 Jung, CW 9/1
70 Grimal, 1991
71 Burkert, 1988
72 ibid
73 ibid
74 ibid
75 Lurker, 1979
76 Riedel, 1986
77 Walker, 1983
78 Burkert, 1988
79 ibid
80 ibid

6 Aggression and lament

81 *Irish Folk-tales* in *Tales of World Literature*, 1969
82 *Handwörterbuch des deutschen Aberglaubens*, 1930
83 For a thorough interpretation of the story, *see* Kast, 1991
84 Grimm's *Fairy Tales*. This translation by M Barton, 1996
85 Kast, 1991

7 The originally positive father complex of the son

86 Gospel of St John, 10,30: 'I and my father are one'
87 König, 1981
88 Kast, 1991
89 Gilligan, 1982
90 Dieckmann, 1991

91 Sheldrake, 1989
92 Kast, 1984
93 Mahler, 1985
94 Bovensiepen, 1987
95 Rhode-Dachser, 1991
96 Jung, CW 10
97 Bovensiepen, 1987
98 Kast, 1993[2]
99 ibid

9 The originally negative mother complex in women

100 Neumann, 1988

10 'As though paralysed'

101 Jacoby, 1985
102 *compare with* Kast, 1992[1]

11 The originally negative father complex in men

103 Kafka, 1978. Translation of these excerpts by M Barton, 1996
104 ibid
105 ibid
106 ibid
107 ibid
108 ibid
109 ibid
110 ibid
111 ibid
112 ibid
113 ibid
114 ibid
115 ibid
116 ibid
117 ibid
118 ibid
119 ibid
120 Emrich, from Kafka, 1978

13 Staking out territory in the unknown

121 Fromm, 1989
122 Haerlin, 1987
123 ibid
124 ibid
125 ibid
126 ibid
127 ibid

Bibliography

Alston, Toni M, 'Mamas kleines Mädchen' in Psyche 42 (6), 1988

Bachmann, Ingeborg, Three Paths to the Sea (trans Gilbert), Holmes and Meier, 1991

Bernardoni, Claudia, and Vera Werder, 'Erfolg statt Karriere' in Bernardoni and Werder (ed), Ohne Seil und Haken. Frauen auf dem Weg nach oben, KG Sauter-Verlag, Munich, 1990

Blos, Peter, 'Freud und der Vaterkomplex' in Journal of the PSA Seminar, Zurich, 1987

Bovensiepen, Gustav, 'Väter – Fragen nach der Identität' in Zeitschrift für Analytische Psychologie 18, 1987

Burkert, Walter, Ancient Mystery Cults, Harvard UP, 1988

Chodorow, Nancy, Reproduction of Mothering, University of California, 1979

Dieckmann, Hans, Methods in Analytical Psychology, Chiron Publications, 1991

Enke, Helmut, 'Beziehung im Fokus. Die ozeanische Beziehung' in Lindauer Texte, Springer, Berlin, 1991

Erikson, Erik, Identity and the Life Cycle, WW Norton, 1994

Flaake, Karin, 'Erst der männliche Blick macht attraktiv' in Psychologie heute, no 11, 1989

Flaake, Karin and Vera King, Weibliche Adoleszenz. Zur Sozialisation junger Frauen, Campus, Frankfurt-am-Main, 1992

Franz, Marie-Louise von, The Problem of the Puer Aeternus, Spring Publications, New York, 1970

——, Der ewige Jüngling, Kosel, Munich, 1987

Freud, Sigmund, The Interpretation of Dreams, Penguin, 1991

Fromm, Erich, 'Der kreative Mensch' in Fromm, Gesamtausgabe, vol 9, Munich, 1989 (1st published 1959)

Gidion, Heidi, Und ich soll immer alles verstehen. Auf den Spuren von Müttern und Töchtern, Herder Frauenforum, Freiburg, 1988

Giera-Krapp, Margitta, 'Konstellationen des gut-bösen Mutterarchetyps bei der Behandlung früher Störungen' in Zeitschrift für Analytisch Psychologie 19, 1988

Gilligan, Carol, *In a Different Voice*, Harvard UP, 1982

Grimal, Pierre, *Dictionary of Classical Mythology*, Penguin, 1991

Grimm Brothers, *Fairy Tales*

Haerlin, Peter, Wie von selbst. *Vom Leistungszwang zur Mühelosigkeit*, Quadriga, Weinheim, Berlin 1987

Hagemann-White, Carol, 'Berufsfindung und Lebensperspektive in der weiblichen Adoleszenz' in Flaake and King, 1992

Hancock, Emily, *The Girl Within*, New York, 1989

Handwörterbuch des deutschen Aberglaubens, ed Hanns Bachtold-Staubli, Berlin, 1930

Hartling, Peter (ed), *Die Väter. Berichte und Geschichten*, Fischer TB, Frankfurt, 1975

Hillmann, James, 'Verrat' in *Zeitschrift für Analytische Psychologie* 10 (2), 1979

Jacoby, Mario, 'Autorität und Revolte – der Mythos vom Vatermord' in *Zeitschrift für Analytische Psychologie* 6, 1975

—— *Individuation und Narzissmus*, Pfeiffer, Munich, 1985

Jung, Carl Gustav, *Collected Works* (CW), ed Read, Fordham and Adler, trans RFC Hull, Routledge and Kegan Paul, London. Reference is made to the following volumes in particular:

CW 2: *Experimental Researches*

CW 3: *The Psychogenesis of Mental Disease*

CW 4: *Freud and Psychoanalysis*

CW 5: *Symbols of Transformation*

CW 8: *The Structure and Dynamics of the Psyche*, particularly 'A Review of Complex Theory'

CW 9/1: *The Archetypes and the Collective Unconscious*, particularly 'Psychological Aspects of the Mother Archetype'

CW 9/2: *Aion. Researches into the Phenomenology of the Self*, particularly 'The Ego'

CW 10: *Civilization in Transition*

CW 15: *The Spirit in Man, Art and Literature*

Kafka, Franz, *Letter to my Father*, Penguin 1978

Kast, Verena: *Das Assoziationsexperiment in der therapeutischen Praxis*, Bonz, Fellbach, 1980

—— *Paare. Beziehungsphantasien oder Wie Götter sich in Menschen spiegeln*, Kreuz, Stuttgart, 1984

—— *Nature of Loving*, Chiron, 1986

—— *Time to Mourn: Growing through the Grief Process*, Daimon Verlag, Switzerland, 1989

—— *Creative Leap: Psychological Transformation through Crisis*, Chiron, 1991

—— *Dynamics of Symbols*, 1992

—— 'Das kollektive Unbewusste und seine Relevanz für Gegenwartsfragen' in Rhode-Dachser, 1992

—— *Die beste Freundin. Was Frauen miteinander haben*, Kreuz, Stuttgart, 1992

—— in Pflüger, Michael (ed), *Das Paar. Mythos und Wirklichkeit*, Walter, Olten, 1988

—— *Through Emotion to Maturity: Psychological Readings of Fairy Tales*, 1993

—— *Animus and Anima: spiritual growth and separation from parental complexes*, Harvest, 1993

—— *Letting Go and Finding Yourself: Separating from your Children*, Continuum Publishing Co, 1994

—— *Fairy Tales as Therapy*, 1995

König, Karl, *Angst und Persönlichkeit. Das Konzept und seine Anwendungen vom steuerndem Objekt*, Vandenhoeck und Ruprecht, Göttingen, 1981

Leonard, Linda, *Tochter und Vater. Heilung einer verletzten Beziehung*, Kosel, Munich, 1985

Lurker, Manfred, *Wörterbuch der Symbolik*, Kroner, Stuttgart, 1979

Mahler, Margaret, *Psychological Birth of the Human Infant. Symbiosis and Individuation*, H Karnac, 1985

Neumann, Erich, *The Child: Structure and Dynamic of the Nascent Personality*, H Karnac, 1988

Nin, Anais, *Journal of a Wife*, P Owen, 1984

Papousek, Mechthild, 'Die Rolle des Vaters in der frühen Kindheit. Ergebnisse der entwicklungsbiologischen Forschung' in *Kind und Umwelt* 54

Rhode-Dachser, Christa, 'Weiblichkeitsparadigmen in der Psychoanalyse' in *Psyche* 44, 1990

—— *Expedition in den dunklen Kontinent. Weiblichkeit im Diskurs der Psychoanalyse*, Springer, Berlin, 1991

Rhode-Daachser, C (ed), *Beschädigungen. Psychoanalytische Zeitdiagnosen*, Vandenhoeck und Ruprecht, Göttingen, 1992

Riedel, Ingrid, *Demeters Suche. Mutter und Tochter*, Kreuz, Zurich, 1986

Samuels, Andrew, *The Plural Psyche. Personality, Morality and the Father*, Routledge, 1989

Scarr, Sandra, *Wenn Mütter arbeiten. Wie Kinder und Beruf sich verbinden lassen*, Beck, Munich, 1987

Sheldrake, Rupert, *Presence of the Past*, Random, 1989

Stern, Daniel, *Diary of a Baby*, Fontana, 1991

Tales of World Literature (*Märchen der Weltliteratur*), Eugen Diederichs Verlag, Munich, 1969

Tellenbach, H (ed), *Das Vaterbild in Mythos und Geschichte*, Kohlhammer, Stuttgart, 1976

Tulving, E, 'Episodic and semantic memory' in E Tulving and W Donaldson (ed), *Organization of Memory*, Academic Press, New York, 1972

Walker, Barbara G, *The Woman's Encyclopedia of Myths and Secrets*, Harper Row, San Francisco, 1983

Zeul, Mechthild, 'Die Bedeutung des Vaters in der weiblichen Entwicklung' in *Psyche* 42 (4), 1988

Index